Jacob's Ladder

Theology and Spirituality in the thought of Austin Farrer

Charles C. Hefling, Jr.

JACOB'S LADDER

JACOB'S LADDER

Theology and Spirituality in the Thought of
Austin Farrer

CHARLES C. HEFLING, JR.

COWLEY PUBLICATIONS
CAMBRIDGE, MASSACHUSETTS
1979

v

To
the people of
Saint Stephen's Memorial Church,
Lynn, Massachusetts,
studying with whom the Revelation of John
first led me to
Austin Farrer

CONTENTS

CONTENTS

PREFACE

MOST BOOKS divulge their authors' real intentions in the subtitle, and this one is no exception. Preacher and metaphysician, poet and biblical scholar, Austin Farrer was an altogether remarkable person and perhaps the most remarkable characteristic of his work is the way it fuses practical religious living and disciplined scholarly thought.

This introduction to Farrer expands and, I hope, improves upon three lectures originally delivered to the American Congregation of the Society of St John the Evangelist in Cambridge. In all of them I have suggested that the same continuity of faith and speculation that animates Farrer's sermons is also the starting-point of his scholarly work and, ultimately, its goal.

Farrer remarks in his first book that laziness is the radical sin of the mind; it is not a sin of which he is guilty. The breadth and depth of his thought make it difficult to explore in a few pages. The scope of his published work is itself impressive, and within a given book or essay he frequently draws together fields and topics that others allow to remain disparate. On the other hand, the thoroughness and wealth of detail with which he supports his arguments is equally remarkable, and sometimes makes for difficult reading. Hoping to avoid the extremes of portraying Farrer as a dilettante or as a narrow specialist, I have tried here both to suggest the outlines of the forest and to present a few specimen trees.

The choice of what to present and what to omit has not been easy. I should have like, for example, to include something of Farrer's interpretation of the book of Revelation, because it is in some ways more successful than his work on the Gospel of Mark, and because *A Rebirth of Images* was my own introduction to his thought. Although he hoped to counteract the tendency to relegate the Revelation of John to the fringes of the New Testament canon, however, Farrer would probably acknowledge that the gospels are more central than the Apocalypse to contemporary Christian belief. Limiting the second lecture to his unique approach to the earliest gospel has still presented problems, and many fine points have had to be omitted.

For Farrer's own books this one is no substitute. My hope is that it may provide the incentive to search out some of the volumes listed in the annotated bibliography. Why read Farrer? There are many reasons. Asked to name a single one, I should say that if I have learned anything from him, it is the mutuality of theology *and* spirituality. That is the foundation of his thought, I believe, and the center of his vision.

I am happy to record my indebtedness to three people who have helped me to see Austin Farrer's work with new eyes: Professor Gordon Kaufman, who rekindled my interest in Farrer; the Reverend Andrew Mead, who first pointed me to *The Glass of Vision;* and Victoria Raymer, from whose sympathetic reading of Farrer's sermons I have learned much. I am also grateful to the Society of St John the Evangelist and the Reverend Paul Wessinger, Superior, for the invitation to lecture from which these pages evolved. Cowley Publications has provided encouragement, patience and editorial skill — all in the person of Cynthia Bell, who took devotion to her multiple task to the point of self-sacrifice and at one stage in this book's odyssey broke her arm on the way to pick up a typescript.

C.C.H.

Cambridge, Mass.
September 1979

INTRODUCTION

IT IS UNHEALTHY that theology has so largely lost
the power to bear directly on the realities of life, having
interposed a conceptual (and institutional) jungle."[1] So
writes the principal of one of England's theological col-
leges. The tension to which he points is not new; it has
been felt by Christians time and again. It is the tension between faith and reason, between religion and philosophy.
What has Athens, Tertullian asked in the second century,
to do with Jerusalem? Of what use are the speculations of
the academy to the life of the Church?

Today the tension appears as a suspicion that theologians, those who engage in reasoned discourse about God,
are in fact talking about something quite different from the
God whom believers worship. It has been pointed out that
for the first six centuries of the Church's life, its theologians were bishops. For nine hundred years after that,
theologians were monks. Since about 1500, theologians
have been university professors. It seems to some that
academic theologians, accustomed to residing in Athens,
have abandoned Jerusalem to its own devices. Between
scholars and believers a conceptual jungle has sprouted.

Must believers make a choice then, a choice of *either*
practical religion *or* disciplined thinking? Certainly there is
evidence that a kind of pious anti-intellectualism is growing. Principal Houlden, on the other hand, would close the
gap rather than widen it. The solution he seeks to a very
real problem is the integration of thought and belief. Cer-

tainly Christians must live their faith, but just as certainly they must think about what they believe in order to do so. And they will be able to look to theologians for help only if theology achieves a breadth of vision that can embrace practical realities along with scholarly insight. On the last page of his book, Houlden admits that comprehensiveness is unfortunately just what modern theologians lack — "apart from him to the memory of whose special gift in this regard this study is therefore dedicated."[2]

The dedication is to Austin Farrer. His was a mind thoroughly at home in Jerusalem as well as Athens, a mind — to use his own words — "in which an entire faith is balanced by a luminous philosophical wisdom."[3] How an entire faith, a thoroughly orthodox Christianity, enters into partnership with a luminous philosophical wisdom that draws on both the great tradition of Western thought and the latest developments in philosophy is the topic taken up in the three lectures that form the core of this book.

§2

Farrer's Athens was Oxford. There he was an undergraduate, and there he was made a Doctor of Divinity. For twenty-five years he was chaplain of Trinity College and for nine more, until his death in 1968, Warden of Keble. Both the number and the variety of his books are impressive. The list begins with a classic study in philosophical theism, *Finite and Infinite*, surely one of the most difficult and most brilliant arguments in the history of English theology. He wrote two Lenten books for the Church of England and several devotional works. He was a poet, too, producing limericks and parodies as well as fine metrical translations of liturgical verse. His biblical studies and commentaries are as provocative as they are out of the ordinary. Of *The Glass of Vision*, Farrer's series of Bampton Lectures, it has been said that "surely St. Mary's had seen and heard nothing like it since John Henry Newman occupied that pulpit."[4]

Yet along with this impressive output, and along with pastoral and administrative duties, Farrer preached regularly. The wonder is that in spite of so many other claims on his energy, nearly all of his published sermons show that he took his responsibilities as a preacher with great seriousness, planning the shortest homily with the same care he gave to his important Hulsean Sermons. According to his editor, Farrer almost never preached except from a full manuscript — fortunately for those who never heard him. Four volumes of these have now been published, three since his death. This is significant in itself, given that sermons are no longer popular reading. Many are the preachers who would be happy to have a single collection worthy of being published. Sermons are of course *spoken* essays in the first place, and how often it happens that a preacher's words, moving or enlightening when heard, lose their power on paper.

Farrer, though, was no ordinary preacher. He has been called one of the great preachers of his generation, and his sermons can be read without evaporating; often a second or third reading uncovers fresh riches. In many ways his preaching displays in miniature the remarkable way Farrer's theology illumines the Christian life and, conversely, the equally remarkable way his spirituality shines in even his most erudite studies. These sermons have been called "weighed and precise statements of theology and spirituality."[5] As such they serve as an excellent introduction to his more extended works. Not that the sermons are easy reading; to take them seriously is to be led into the deep mysteries of human existence and divine love.

The sermons embrace theology *and* spirituality. This *and* is a pivot on which all of Farrer's many-sided thought turns. The preacher and the theologian were one and the same person, and to turn from Farrer's sermons to his theological works is to see the details and the background — but nothing essentially different. And, "weighed and precise" though they are, Farrer's sermons are by no means impersonal. There is no biography yet, although one is now being written, but his interests and parts of his history can be glimpsed in the allusions he builds into his preaching.

Farrer's father was a Baptist minister, who put him "in the way of knowing God, and then stood out of the light of that ray which comes from heaven, and which no man, even the dearest of fathers, can communicate."[6] Together, father and son built an oak fence one summer when Farrer, his eyes ruined by poring over Greek texts for an examination, had been forbidden to read. It is typical that from this human incident flows a sermon on the most superhuman of mysteries, the Trinity of persons in God.

Farrer tells in another sermon how his conversion to the Church of England began one Sunday when, at a friend's invitation, he visited a parish church in Oxford. He was an undergraduate then; returning years later to the same church to preach at their dedication festival, he recalled his experience:

> The way of worship was new to me . . . I was much moved by it. My friend and I walked away afterwards and said nothing. When we were about half-way home, however, we ventured to exchange a remark or two. We agreed upon a formula. 'There were angels in the roof,' we said. So after that we were always in your church.[7]

To be an Anglican was for Farrer to be a Catholic — always with a capital C — but he insisted as well that his was Reformed Christianity. He gave his loyalty to the Church and not to any party, and even the Church he loved only as a means. A clever child with a telescope, he suggests, may begin by making a fuss over the tubes and lenses, and Christians may begin by making a fuss about the Church. But just as the purpose of any optical instrument is to eliminate itself, to become transparent, leaving the viewer face to face with the object of vision, so too the Church, its creeds and sacraments, exists only as a glass of vision that lets Christ be seen.

So Farrer agreed with a certain military widow who once said to him about the rites of the Church that "if these things are done, they want doing smartly," but he had no desire to undo the Reformation, and he declared himself uncomfortable whenever he was asked to take part in "the intricate and absolutely dead etiquette of the Old Constantinople . . . draped around the supper of the Lord."[8] As *The Crown of the Year* and the sermons composed for delivery at the eucharist show, his sacramental piety was deep, but that is because he knew that through the eucharist he touched a living Christ. This alone mattered; never liturgy as such.

Similarly, the Bible is a mirror of things divine. Farrer often preaches on scriptural texts; he preaches, that is, through them rather than about them. The most unexpected lectionary assignments lead him to central Christian themes. From Elisha and the widow's pot of oil (2 Kg. 4:2) he moves to the difference between forms of worship and the Spirit who fills those forms, and from there to the believer's own life as a member of the body of Christ, the Spirit-filled vessel of grace. This sermon concludes with Farrer's suggestions for personal prayer and (as was his nearly invariable custom) with an ascription of praise to the Trinity. The story of Saul and the witch of Endor (1 Sam. 28:7) leads him to consider the universal Cause who is God, the discernment of God's will for this present life, the fellowship of Christ's passion, and the power of his resurrection.

Sometimes Farrer starts by examining his text, especially if it is a passage so important or well-known that no introduction is necessary; or, on the other hand, if it is particularly difficult. Occasionally he dwells on a text throughout the sermon, bringing to bear on it the results of his detailed New Testament studies. Most often Farrer begins in a commonplace way, with Beatrix Potter's animal drawings, for example, or a student's motorcar painted in four bright colors, or his experiences as a gardener. He tells about his aunts, of whom there were quite a few; they lived together in a house known to their nieces and nephews as the Aunt Heap. And he reveals that his good friend, the theologian Eric Mascall, once beat a computer that had been programmed to play infallible chess.

"In the year of grace 1929 (always allowing that I remember correctly) I dropped my spoon into my soup." So begins a sermon on responsibility for friends. "The mole, for example, is a quaint and agreeable beast: I have sometimes met him taking a walk, but I have not cultivated his acquaintance." So begins "Trinity of Love" — one of Farrer's best sermons. On careful scrutiny the four collections divulge that he was once a scoutmaster, that he relished Shakespeare, that he was tied for thirteenth place among fifteen competitors in a certain mathematical examination, and that he went to theological college with Michael Ramsey, later archbishop of Canterbury.

§3

Farrer disapproves, however, of preachers who use the pulpit for confessions or for autobiography. His own life provides anecdotes and illustrations, but for models of Christian living he turns to others. One of his aunts, for instance, went to live at the Aunt Heap only after having been a missionary doctor in India until her seventieth year. Farrer describes her sense of calling, her patience in testing and following it, the hospitals she built from her own designs, the daunting conditions under which she worked, and ends, simply, "there have been more Christians like this than some of you realize." Another example, who like his "little Aunt" appears more than once in Farrer's preaching, is a man who had been with him at his theological college. Formerly an engineer, Hugh Lister decided to devote his life to overcoming the estrangement of ordinary workers from the gospel. He worked in a tough London parish; he worked for organized labor; the story goes on. What is its message? "The will of God! that was what my friend cared for. He just cared about it: he did not make himself care."[9]

God's likeness in men and women is a constant theme of Farrer's preaching, and "In His Image" is the title of his commemorative sermon on C.S. Lewis, who appears in other sermons as well. Lewis and Farrer were Oxford dons together for twenty-five years, from Farrer's appointment to the chaplaincy of St Edmund Hall to Lewis's departure for Cambridge. Both were active participants in the Socratic Club which Lewis helped to found for the purpose of discussing Christianity. Sometimes their interests in certain questions overlapped. Lewis's essay "Myth Became Fact," for example, appeared a few months before Farrer's "Can Myth be Fact?" Lewis dedicated his *Reflections on the*

Psalms to Austin and Katherine Farrer, and his esteem for Farrer glows in the preface he wrote for *A Faith of Our Own*, the American edition of Farrer's first volume of sermons. Besides the memorial address, Farrer wrote an appreciative (but not uncritical) essay, called "The Christian Apologist," for the collection *Light on C.S. Lewis.* He admired Lewis's interplanetary fantasies, although his own imagination took a more terrestrial turn. The difference appears humorously in one of the many bursts of his own verse that brighten Farrer's writing:

> *Go aboard. I will leave you and Lewis in orbit;*
> *With him for your pilot, perhaps you'll*
> *Encounter the Martian mind, and absorb it;*
> *I'm backing to earth in my capsule.*[10]

What did Austin Farrer find most praiseworthy in C.S. Lewis? It was that Lewis could think about all that he strongly felt, and feel the realities about which he thought. Not to overwork the comparison, it can be said that an integration not unlike this gives strength to Farrer's own work: it is not surprising that he could recognize it in others.

His colleague Basil Mitchell has said that Farrer's intention and effect was always to direct one's gaze *away* from himself, and *to* whatever was the object of his attention.[11] His aptly-chosen stories and figures of speech add interest and woo the reader, but in Farrer's sermons they serve larger purposes. Everyday occurrences are used to proclaim and explore supernatural truth. Whatever their source, commonplace incidents soon give way to the great images of Christianity, and presently the reader finds what Farrer himself found in St Paul's letters: that his "feet have gone through the floor and his head through the roof, and that he is speaking in the large dimension of inspired vision."[12] Carrying his readers from natural to supernatural reality, from the world to God, was a task he set himself whether he was composing sermons, or analyzing the symbols of the Apocalypse, or probing the mystery of freewill.

Because the sermons show this process taking place within a small compass, it is easy to overlook the enormous scholarship that lies beneath their surface. Farrer does not lead us on a tour of the kitchen, or describe the ingredients, or detail the steps of the recipe. He offers a meal for the soul. The preliminary work has been done, however, and it makes itself felt without being obvious. Farrer preached well, not in spite of his academic credentials and accomplishments, but because of them — a combination as valuable as it is rare. Although his genius is distilled and applied in the sermons, the refined product still has a recognizable continuity with the scholarly books and essays. Its solid theological and philosophical groundwork is an important part of the durability, the timeless quality that many have found in Farrer's preaching.

Although he is always specific and concrete in his thinking, he is seldom topical. Those who seek after news in any of his books will be disappointed. There is, Farrer admits, "nothing in these pages about nuclear bombs, artificial insemination, free love, world government, Church reunion, or the restyling of public worship."[13] Not that he denies the practical implications of Christian faith. Belief, he insists, must be lived, but the basis of that lived belief is personal relationship to a personal God. Mitchell, who knew him well, writes that Farrer can be called unworldly only in the sense that "he was almost entirely indifferent to and largely unaffected by the world in which reputations are made, movements initiated, influences received or imparted. Using the word broadly, he had no *political* interests."[14]

That is perhaps a weakness of the sermons. If so, it is compensated by Farrer's understanding of and sympathy with the problem of living one's belief in the sphere of individual choices and personal relationships. He does not merely recommend prayer; he gives examples, and he urges consultation with a priest as best of all. What else, he asks, are the clergy for? His sermons on particular virtues and vices — pride, responsibility to friends, candor, caprice, chastity, Lenten duty, money, commitment — are anything but vague. They are disquietingly specific in their rebukes and their prescriptions alike.

Inevitably, some of the sermons reflect the situations of undergraduates, to whom the majority were preached. These, however, are few. Farrer preached the same gospel to the University of Oxford, the congregation at a marriage, the monastic community of the Cowley Fathers, and the alumni of St Paul's School. His spiritual counsels about making a retreat or beginning to pray are applicable to all sorts and conditions of Christians. There is, he writes repeatedly, only one relation of the human person to God. The divine will is everywhere present; it is a question of how to find it and embrace it.

"The will of God" is a phrase that Farrer uses constantly, and "willing the will of God" is as much the essence of his theology as of his preaching. The definition of God that he develops in his philosophical theology is that God is all he wills to be, and wills to be all that he is. It might be surprising to find this definition appearing also in his sermons; surprising, that is, if it seemed out of place. But it does not, so deftly is that idea tied to the topics on which he is preaching. The reverse is also true, for the practical concerns of believers are never absent from even the most subtle of Farrer's intellectual arguments. It is not strange to find him introducing the practice, not just the concept, of prayer as one of the links in a chain of reasoning by which he argues philosophically for God's existence.

Farrer did not confuse practical religion with theoretical theology, but neither did he separate them, still less oppose them. His books are all of a piece, so that the sermons throw light on the philosophy, the biblical studies on the devotional works, and so on throughout his writing. *The Glass of Vision* is probably the most striking example of this wholeness. Its eight lectures cover an amazing range of scholarly topics, and each of them concludes with the same Trinitarian ascriptions Farrer uses in Sunday sermons.

Thus the gradual transition in a sermon from the mole, that "quaint and agreeable beast," to the life of God which is above all worlds has its exemplar in Farrer's "natural" theology. It is a special case of seeing one of God's creatures as a clue to its Creator, a case of glimpsing the Almighty through his works. To ponder and clarify that movement, climbing through the natural order to its source, is one of theology's tasks. "But now," Farrer would add, "I am sorry I said we have to climb, for love has come down to us, the heart of heaven is here."[15] On this opposite movement, the unimaginable condescension whereby the Creator comes to be born in a stable, theology also reflects.

> We should all be agnostics if our knowledge of God were our exploration of him; as though God sat there impassive as a rock-cut Buddha, and we tortoises vainly tried to scale his knees. We cannot aspire to talk about God in (as it were) divine language, but he can stoop, if he chooses, to talk to us in our language and to deal humanly with mankind.[16]

To start from creation is "natural" theology; to start from Christ, "revealed" theology. Both are concerned with how we come to know God and speak about him, and each is inseparable from the other.

Farrer has a favorite image for this two-way relationship between the finite and the Infinite. He compares it to the ladder, set up between earth and heaven, on which Jacob in his dream at Bethel saw angels climbing up and down (Gen. 28:10–22). The image of Jacob's ladder appears in the metaphysical complexities of *Finite and Infinite*, in the sermons, and in Farrer's poetry. Theology and spirituality travel in both directions, through the human aspiration that seeks God and through the divine inspiration that draws the minds of men and women.

The first of the three lectures that follow presents Farrer's natural or, as he prefers to say, rational theology. It concentrates on what he understands by "proving" God's existence in relation to the reasons believers actually have for making assertions that imply the existence of a creative providence. The second lecture deals with what Farrer sometimes calls "scriptural divinity," his study of the products of inspired thinking that constitute the Christian scriptures.

Because Farrer is sometimes known as primarily a philosopher, sometimes as primarily a New Testament scholar, the third lecture endeavors to show that he was both, and that the interaction of rational and revealed theology is essential to his thoughtful Christian faith.

I

THROUGH A GLASS
IN A RIDDLE

---

*For now we see through a glass, darkly; but then face
to face: now I know in part; but then shall I know
even as also I am known.* I CORINTHIANS, XIII. 12

HOW DO WE RECOGNIZE GOD? St Paul's answer
in I Corinthians, very literally translated, is that we
see only "through a glass in a riddle." It is one of Austin
Farrer's favorite texts. The motif of an enigmatic mirror, a
glass of riddles, runs like a thread through the whole fabric
of his thought. It turns up in sermons and essays, and provides the title for perhaps his most important book, *The
Glass of Vision.* What we can see of God in this life, we
glimpse "through a glass in a riddle." Still to come is the
beatific vision of God face to face. Meanwhile, the knowledge that finite creatures achieve is indirect; it shines
through a glass. And to know God is to know that he is infinitely beyond our knowing. We know him in our questioning as much as in our always meagre answers; God is
known *in a riddle.*

Glass and riddle suggest, respectively, the medium through which divine activity comes into awareness, and the means by which that awareness is grasped. To know God is to apprehend him through something that is not God, and to conceive him by means of human thoughts that are always inadequate. Farrer finds the mirror, that finite clue to the infinite God, in the soul; that is, in the higher functions of personal activity that characterize the "spiritual" part of human nature. Divine truth, he proposes, makes itself known through "what is highest, most central, most characteristic of the human mind."[1] The unraveling of the riddle is the mode of thinking called theology.

As the introduction suggests, Farrer distinguishes what we can "naturally" know about God from what depends upon God's "supernatural" act of disclosing himself. Accordingly theology has two branches, or two distinct but closely related tasks. Farrer uses the term "rational theology" for the working-out of the awareness of God's activity in the natural world. Rational theology is more general than, and in some sense prior to, theology derived from God's specific revelation. This does not mean for Farrer that there is access to divine truth in and through unaided reason, but he does find a legitimate place for what tradition calls the preambles of faith. Reason in theology is never "unaided"; rational theology as Farrer understands it cannot be a purely human activity, in contrast to a purely divine activity called revelation. Instead, the rational theologian reflects on and reasons about the experience, common to many traditions, of God's activity by way of nature.

Within Christianity, rational theology in Farrer's sense is therefore closely linked with the doctrine of God's creative providence, the teaching that through God's will all things were created and have their being. Certainly "natural" knowledge of God never stands alone. It is supplemented — but not supplanted — by the good news revealed in Christ. A difference there is, but to use the simple terms "reason" and "revelation" makes too sharp a distinction. Farrer stresses a continuity between the two, and prefers to speak of *natural* reason and *supernatural* revelation. We ought, he writes in *The Glass of Vision,*

> to throw the emphasis on the adjectives rather than upon the nouns. We have not to distinguish between God's action and ours, but between two phases of God's action — his supernatural action, and his action by way of nature.[2]

§2

This lecture considers Farrer's rational theology. It is a more difficult topic than that of "scriptural divinity," which is taken up in the second lecture. Rational theology means reasoned thinking that calls on all the resources of philosophy including, for Farrer, metaphysical theology. At its core are arguments for theism. The first order of business, that is, lies in what has usually (and misleadingly) been called the philosophical proof of God's existence.

But is this not a very unpromising way to begin a discussion whose theme is theology *and* spirituality? If there is anything that deserves to be called a "conceptual jungle," anything with as little bearing as possible on the soul's health, is it not the arid and superfluous notion of theistic proof? Anyone who is up on philosophy knows that the thing cannot be done. Even if it could, must we not say with Pascal that the God of the philosophers is not the God of Abraham, Isaac and Jacob?

These are legitimate questions. But the first thing to notice is that they already presuppose that there is a gap between philosophy and faith. It is true that not every believer is a philosopher, but it is also true that believers are men and women — that is, they are rational animals — and so they may in fact raise the very questions rational theology addresses. So they too may be disturbed by doubts and criticisms raised on the other side of the gap. Even if Farrer does not attempt to close the gap altogether, he at least tries to narrow it. His rational theology does not grow out of nostalgia for the medieval scholasticism so badly shaken by the Enlightenment; none of his writing attempts to return to the thirteenth century. At bottom, he holds that God is better served by thinking through the difficult questions philosophy poses to belief than by ignoring them.

Early in his life, Farrer became convinced that there is something in the old scholastic arguments. He was, as he puts it, "possessed by the Thomist vision, and could not think it false. The core of the doctrine must somehow be sound, only it must be freed from the period trash in which it was embedded."[3] Moreover, to argue for God's existence is not only possible, it is also a necessity implicit in Christianity. Christians are theists; they worship and obey the Maker of heaven and earth, of all things, seen and unseen. What is the basis for such a belief? It is the universe of beings each of which declares the glory of God and shows his handiwork. An argument for God's existence is not so different from the joyful recognition of creative power that issues in the ancient hymn calling on all the works of the Lord to praise him and magnify him forever. Theistic proof is not fundamentally different, with this qualification: we must understand what "proving" means. Everything turns on that word.

To illustrate what he does *not* mean by proof, Farrer tells a parable based on a childhood adventure story. A party of Roundheads, traveling through a mountain pass, are held up by a hostile Cavalier marksman. While they keep his attention occupied up front, the Roundheads send one of their number stealthily behind to creep up on the Cavalier and ambush him from the rear. "It is commonly supposed by the public," Farrer continues, "and used to be supposed by philosophers, that something of the same sort should take place in our proving the existence of God." First, Religion sights its divine Object by something called faith. But because it cannot be quite sure of this Object, Religion sends Philosophy around by a very different path, the path of reason. When at length Philosophy has crept up on its quarry and discovered God, it can wave a flag at Religion, signaling that all is well. Religion is free to go on enjoying its Object with certainty and good conscience.[4]

That is how rational theology works, if proving means inescapable demonstration. An attempt is made to derive theological conclusions from non-theological premises, dramatically producing the rabbit of theistic proof from the hat of impartial philosophy. Carefully avoiding anything that seems at all pious, the supposedly neutral reasoner builds up a purely intellectual case; then, suddenly, "bang goes the pistol, and therefore, we say, God!"[5] It is schemes like that, however, which finally satisfy neither the believer nor the philosopher. Farrer will have none of it. When he speaks of proving, he means something besides inescapable demonstration. Often he prefers to speak of argument, rather than proof; when he does use "proving," the word has something of its older meaning, which is "testing." The proper analogy, in other words, is not proving a geometrical thesis but proving cannon. To prove a cannon was to try it by firing a charge, so as to be sure the barrel would not break. To prove God's existence is not to create belief, but to test the assumptions believers make. In both cases, there is something to be tested and a reason for testing it.

Before considering what theistic argument tests, and how the testing proceeds, it will be appropriate to ask *why* examining the grounds for belief in God is necessary or even appropriate. How does the question addressed by rational theology arise in the first place? There are several places to begin the discussion. Three that Farrer considers are these:

(1) Suppose I say, "I believe in God." Someone may, without intending to be hostile, ask me *why* I believe. It is a question I may even ask of myself. It can, however, be divided into two further questions, depending on what shade of meaning "why" is given. "Why do I believe?" may be asking about the factors in my life that led me to belief. If so, an autobiographical answer is called for, and I may say, for example, that I believe in God because I have been taught to do so. I did not invent or discover the whole complex of words and actions that give shape to my belief, for they were passed on to me by others — parents or pastors, authors or acquaintances. Presumably that is how belief begins for everyone; religious belief is, among other things, a social phenomenon.

Eventually and gradually, however, we make the beliefs we inherit our own. If we continue to believe and to grow in our faith, then it will be because the words we learned from others really mean something. We will, in other words, have reasons for continuing to say, "I believe in God," and for thinking that our belief makes a difference in our daily life. It is here that the second question arises. "Why do I believe in God?" will come to have a different meaning, one that is more like, "What grounds do I have for thinking that there is a God?" This second meaning of "why" calls for another sort of answer. What is now required is a statement of whatever evidence there may be for taking the notion of God seriously. And this is where rational theology begins, for its task as Farrer understands it is to clarify those reasons that believers entertain.

(2) Perhaps, however, I decide to refine my first statement. By faith in God, I now prefer to say, I mean something that is more like trust in a person than belief in a proposition. Believing is not so much a matter for my head as for my heart. When I say, "I believe in God," I mean that I trust God to fulfill his promises. No doubt that is a more appropriate way to speak. Yet trusting another person presupposes that person's existence; when I trust my doctor, I assume that "my doctor" designates a real being. I may very well trust God if he exists, but how can I trust him *to* exist? It seems that I must have some idea of who it is I trust, and some reasons to think this idea tolerably accurate. That notion and those reasons are what rational theology tests.

(3) This leads to a third way in which the question about the existence of God can arise. Suppose I say that the real center of my believing is prayer. To say "I believe in God" is first and foremost an act of worship, and its proper context is the recitation of the creeds. But does not the very meaning of prayer involve implicitly an affirmation of the One to whom prayer is addressed? If there is no God to be worshiped, then prayer is nothing more than talking to ourselves. It may have some value as a sort of mental tension-reliever or a psychic aspirin to be nibbled when the pain becomes severe — but that is hardly what Christians think of worship. "You may hold that prayer is the highest wisdom or the flimsiest folly," Farrer observes, "but in any case the assertion of God's existence is integral to it."[6]

In all three cases the point is this: belief *in* involves belief *that*. Even when belief in God is understood primarily as an attitude of trust or worship, it still contains the affirmation that God *is*. Believers assume God's existence and get on with the more important business of loving him, but it goes without saying that there has never been a lack of sceptical objections to their assumption. There are any number of amateur and professional philosophers who think they can convince believers that belief in God is meaningless. There are psychologists and biologists, too, who would explain that what is called belief in God is all in the believer's subconscious, or all in his genes.

The believer can of course reply, and rightly, that "the gospel offers God to me as good, not simply as fact. In embracing the good I am convinced of the fact."[7] Rational theology says nothing different, but it may be able to defend this conviction and thereby offer sceptics a rebuttal. This use of argument is called apologetics, and Farrer engages in his share of it; it is not, however, his principal interest. To reason toward God through the evidence of the created order need not be defensive. It is, on the contrary, a way of thinking that comes naturally even without external challenges. Raising questions is the privilege of reasonable beings, and questioning is not the same as doubting. Quite spontaneously, ordinary people do the thinking that theologians regulate and solidify; consequently, in Farrer's estimation, there will be theology just as long as there is religious thinking.

§3

So far, two of Farrer's preliminary concerns have been considered. The first is that arguments for theism do not rest on a source of knowledge that is different from concrete, practical belief; the second, that although faith is far more than an assertion of God's existence, it still includes that assertion. Theology is no independent route. It does not head God off at the pass, as the Roundheads did the Cavalier. As a rational theologian, Farrer weighs the reasons believers really have, although most of us are less adept than he at putting those reasons into words. Rational theology is neither a substitute for belief, nor the same thing as belief; it is "examining or articulating the assumptions of the believing mind."[8]

It follows that Farrer cannot entertain the idea that God is merely the inference at the end of a chain of logical reasoning. However dark or riddling, we do have some awareness of God prior to our thinking, some interaction with him about which, not to which, we reason. Indeed, a God about whom we can do nothing but think would be no God at all. What theology considers, then, is the active relation of God to his creatures, a relation that is presumably everywhere, could we but recognize it.

If modern philosphers find statements about this relationship doubtful, Farrer suggests that the problem is not that they are "suffering from too much logic, but from too little contemplation."[9] Theology, even metaphysical theology, is always in some way contemplative and for Farrer, it is not unlike an act of devotion. How could it be otherwise, if theology's purpose is to examine and prolong a genuine movement of the human spirit from finite to Infinite? For all its "period trash," the medieval approach at its best never lost the conviction that God can be honored intellectually; in its own way, Farrer's reflective theism carries on that tradition in which theology explores the ascent of the heart and mind to God.

It would be inappropriate to overwork a comparison between his approach to theology and that of an almost mystical thinker like Bonaventure, but none the less there are some striking parallels. Writing in a far more secular age, Farrer at times follows a path not unlike the one Bonaventure took in the thirteenth century in his *Itinerarium Mentis in Deum*. The title can only be translated today as *The Soul's Journey into God*, but literally it means "the mind's journey." We make a rather sharp distinction today, but mind and soul were not separate for Bonaventure. For him, as for Farrer, mental activity is one part of human spirituality.

Bonaventure uses Jacob's ladder, one of Farrer's favorite images, to symbolize the pilgrimage toward loving God with all the mind. *The Soul's Journey* passes through successive stages of meditation on the natural world. Each step draws closer to the God who nevertheless remains infinitely above human conceptualization; each makes clearer the dark vision through the mirror of the world. The first three rungs of Bonaventure's ladder constitute a kind of natural theology. First, "since we must ascend Jacob's ladder before we descend it, let us place our initial step in the ascent at the bottom, presenting to ourselves the whole material world as a mirror through which we may pass over to God, the supreme Craftsman."

All that is, seen and unseen, is the basis from which Bonaventure takes a first step. The universe is "itself a ladder by which we can ascend to God," for it "proclaims the divine power that produces all things . . . and the divine goodness that lavishly adorns them." This first step must be followed by another, because "the mirror presented by the external world is of little or no value unless the mirror of our soul is cleansed and polished." There is a second step, then, at "the point of reentering into ourselves, that is, into our mind, where the divine image shines forth."

In the second stage, Bonaventure considers human consciousness, by which alone the external world becomes transparent.

The third stage is reached "not only by passing through ourselves but also *in* ourselves." There is an internal ladder, a scale of degrees of excellence within the human spirit; accordingly, Bonaventure considers that contemplation at this third level is more valuable than the previous two. The world displays the supreme Craftsman's work, but in human beings his image is more perfectly realized, and finally what is highest and most Godlike in humanity also ascends most closely to the divine. This "summit of the mind," the top of the interior ladder, is "the spark of conscience," which Bonaventure understands as the natural tendency of men and women towards goodness. Corresponding to this threefold movement, our mind has three orientations. The first is outward, toward exterior or material objects; the second orientation of the mind is within itself and into itself; the third is "above itself."[10]

By these three stages the journey into God begins. The next section will draw some comparisons between Farrer's arguments and the plan of these early chapters of Bonaventure's book. Here it should be pointed out that *The Soul's Journey*, although it is not at all a logical demonstration, is nevertheless a quest for knowledge of God through the effects of his activity in nature. Certainly Bonaventure insists that the quest will fail unless it is preceded by prayer and repentance; it depends, too, on an attitude towards the created order that seeks to understand rather than to control or exploit. Nothing could be further than this second condition from the twentieth century's effort to master nature by technology.

The loss of a contemplative appetite for what really is, Farrer thinks, can only mean the death of the soul. "For religion is based on respect for being — for God, yes, but only because God is seen to be uniquely worthy of it by a mind open to respect for being in general."[11] If such a respectful frame of mind is matched by a thirst for understanding, the result is likely to be philosophical theology, which to the end of his career Farrer held to be a concern for what things are, and not for how they look or how they can be manipulated.

Farrer shares with Bonaventure not only a general attitude, but a manner of proceeding as well. Although he made important modifications, the outline of his argument remains much the same. God Is Not Dead, published two years before Farrer's death, shows it clearly. Like Bonaventure in The Soul's Journey, Farrer begins by considering "the whole material world." He then narrows the scope to examine human existence, a particular but privileged subset of the natural order. The crucial point is his concentration, within human being, on an interior, conscious scale.

Clearly these three stages are similar to Bonaventure's as outlined above, and the resemblance is more than superficial. On the issue that separates Bonaventure from his contemporary Thomas Aquinas, Farrer sides with the former. For Bonaventure our awareness of the world as changeable, imperfect, or finite depends upon a notion we already possess, however vaguely, of a Being that is eternal, perfect, and infinite. God is present to us in our thinking about God itself, not only at the end of the journey but along with every step. In a similar vein, Farrer speaks of the "light and liberation" that came to him when he found that he could understand God "as the underlying cause of my thinking, especially of those thoughts in which I tried to think of him."[12]

§4

To think about God is to think about his activity. What does God do? Fundamental to Christian theism is the idea of God as the Creator who providentially orders all that is, who holds the universe in being and guides it towards its proper end. The ascent of Jacob's ladder can therefore quite appropriately begin with the cosmos, the "whole material world," as Bonaventure puts it. What we think of the cosmos determines whether or not we take the first step, for the difference between believer and unbeliever, theist and atheist, appears even at this first and most basic level. Farrer puts the matter this way: "The atheist's ultimate fact is the world; the theist's ultimate fact is God."[13]

No one who seriously thinks that the universe is the last word is likely to be persuaded by Farrer's arguments — or by any others. If the world strikes us as nothing but brute fact, if it does not even raise a question about where it comes from or where it is going, what reason is there even to begin to look beyond the world for answers? The question comes first, for Farrer thinks that to swallow the brute facticity of things is much the same as to denounce from the start the whole idea of ultimate explanation, which is the idea of an omnipotent Cause.

Some people, though, are not content simply to accept brute "thereness." The novelist Evelyn Waugh humorously describes the plight of such a person in his lapsed parson, Mr. Prendergast. It was business as usual, Prendergast tells us, "when suddenly, for no reason at all, my *Doubts* began." His was not "the ordinary sort of Doubt about Cain's wife or the Old Testament miracles or the consecration of Archbishop Parker." It was something deeper.

Prendergast was mystified by one question — why is there a world at all? "Once granted the first step, I can see that everything else follows — Towel of Babel, Babylonian captivity, Incarnation, Church, bishops, incense, everything — but what I couldn't see, and what I can't see now, is, *why* did it all begin?"[14]

Mr. Prendergast's "doubts" unfortunately led him to give up religion, but at least the question "why is it so?" had some force in his mind. He did not take the world as brute fact, and that might have led him back to belief. To raise questions about why things are the way they are is already to have a toehold on Jacob's ladder. Questions about the world's origin are not yet, in themselves, theism. Yet they do indicate what Farrer calls "crypto-theism," the mental unrest that looks for explanations. The world is a riddle; it sets us wondering why it is as it is, and Farrer defines a theist as one "who does full justice to the question 'Why is it so?' "[15]

The answer to this very large riddle is not immediately apparent. It may be that believers are convinced that the world *is* because God wills it to be, but that is just the assumption that is under scrutiny. The heavens declared the glory of God to the ancient psalmist, but if they declare it today they do so indirectly at best. We live with astronomy, and Farrer observes that while astronomy raises our wonder about origins, still it does nothing to satisfy it. So it is with every other feature of the natural order. "If we ask whether nature reveals God, the answer will be Yes and No. Yes, for nature presents us with a vast extent of God's physical and creative thought; it gives us evidence for the enormous scope and intimate subtlety of his wisdom." So far, Farrer's words echo Bonaventure. But the answer must also be no, he continues, "for nature fails to supply the essential clue by which her own signs can be read."[16]

The creation, in other words, indicates its Creator only if it is read aright; that is, if it is read *as* a creation, as an effect and not as a brute fact. It is too simplistic to reason that the world needs an explanation, and the only act that could cause the assembly of beings we call the world to *be* — not just to be this or that, but to exist — is the act of an infinite Will. God's act of creation explains why anything and everything is. This inference may be correct, and for Farrer it is correct, but its premise needs to be elaborated. If people come to feel in their bones that the world is not capable of operating on its own, if they read the world not as an ultimate fact but as a riddle, the important question is *why* they come to think that way.

It is, after all, a rather strange way to think, since in the first place, no one experiences "the" world. Farrer insists that in fact there is no such thing:

> The universe isn't *an* organism or *a* system or *a* process: it's an unimaginable free-for-all of innumerable bits of organism, system, process; or, if you'll allow me an antiquated piece of slang, it's not a thing, it's just one damned thing after another.[17]

If we regard the world as a riddle, it is most likely that we have found one part of it, one of the bits of free-for-all, to be inexplicable in itself. From that starting-point, it is natural to expand the insight. Eventually we may arrive at the conclusion that every thing, every instance of finite being, depends on something outside itself to account for its occurrence or to explain why it is. Such a starting-point will be the clue by which we read the world's riddle.

So the more significant question, and the one on which Farrer concentrates, is not "why does the world exist?" but "why does any entity exist?" Why does existence itself need to be accounted for? Why does such a curious question as "why is it so?" arise at all? These riddles mark a second step of the ladder. Farrer's way of addressing the puzzled Mr. Prendergast might be something like this. You want to know why the world exists, why it came to be in the first place? Very well, you must then have some idea of what "existing" means. Where did you come by it? Is there a particular case of existing that especially needs to be explained, so that it sets in motion this whole rather odd way of thinking, and makes it reasonable to ask what causes things to be?

To these invented queries Farrer gives the answer himself. If we wonder about the existence of the world, or about the existence of any part of the world, it is because we *experience* what existing is. We experience it directly, in ourselves. That is the indispensable clue. To say that the world needs to be explained means that existing as such is not self-explanatory, and that can be said only on the basis of the one kind of existing with which we are directly acquainted — our own. When this clarification is made, the difference between the atheist and the theist comes down to this: one denies, the other affirms, that human existence has a superhuman Source.

What is it, then, about our first-hand acquaintance with existence that demands to be explained? It is our experience of our own limitation, our finitude in the special theological sense, and it is this that Farrer endeavors to make clear. What does it mean, first, to say that I am "acquainted" with what I am? There are a number of ways in which it can be said that I exist. What I *am*, depending on the point of view, is a bundle of chemicals, or a biological organism, or a maze of subconscious desires and attitudes. Yet my being cannot be reduced to any of those aspects, and in any case I can experience none of them directly.

Where I do experience my own being is in what I do. I exist, this moment, in my own present activity. The chemical, biological, or psychological facts about me enter into my active existence, but do not completely explain it.

When he speaks of experiencing our own activity as limited, therefore, Farrer does not just mean the limitations imposed by our physical or psychic make-up. No doubt we are limited in those ways, but finitude in the theological sense means more. Farrer examines instead two further kinds of limitation that are relevant, two ways in which the activity we experience in ourselves is constrained. In the first place, I am limited by what I cannot do. I may do my best to keep a ten o'clock appointment, but I simply cannot do so if, at nine fifty-nine, I am a mile away and on foot. As Farrer puts it, "when I find how many things I cannot do, I am simply realizing that I am Austin Farrer, and not God Almighty, not even the Archangel Gabriel, nor even Immanuel Kant, nor even the captain of university athletics."[18]

To realize one's limitation in this sense may, of course, be a cause for wonder. Almost everyone at some time or other has fallen into a certain amazement when considering why it is that, as Gilbert and Sullivan's song says,

> in spite of all temptations
> to belong to other nations,
> he remains an Englishman

or, for that matter, a person of some other specific time and place. Historical particularity is finitude of a certain kind, yet it does not mirror the Creator so clearly as another set of limitations which are of more interest to Farrer. My free activity is not only limited by what I cannot do; I am limited as well in my doing of what I can.

In part, this is simply another way of saying that I can only do one thing at a time. When I choose my actions, it is always a concrete choice between this and that, an active preference of one activity over another. What I can do is limited by the fact that whenever I make a choice, I cut myself off from any number of alternatives. I *can* write the next of these lectures; I *can* take a nap. Both are activities of which I am capable, but tomorrow I may have to choose which of them will be actualized. Which, I must decide, will enter the pattern of my active being and become part of who I am? No matter which I choose, my existing will have gone forward. I shall have carried on the business of being, and done so in a particular, limited or finite manner.

This ability to choose between alternatives that are real possibilities is the essence of my freewill. Nothing is more central to Farrer's thought than his insistence that the actions by which we become the kind of beings we are cannot be explained by anything else in the world. They are free actions. Fourteen of the fifteen chapters in *The Freedom of the Will* are devoted to defending this conviction. It is crucial to uphold the reality of voluntary activity because "it is only in being aware of something finite as an analogy of God that we begin to be aware of God at all."[19] To speak of everything that is as "created" depends upon having a standard instance that gives meaning to the verb "create." Farrer's standard instance is the existence that we create. Here and here alone is there activity that is more than just a rearrangement of what already is, activity that is truly new. In free action, therefore, Farrer argues that we experience directly an aspect of the natural order that is suited to symbolize God's creative action. What does God do as Creator? He does something similar to, though infinitely more than, what I do when I create myself. That is the beginning of theistic thought.

Before considering why human creativity leads us to think that there is such a thing as divine creativity, it will be well to review the steps taken so far. With the existence of the cosmos as its starting-point, Farrer's argument proceeds to consider human activity as part of the cosmos, and from there narrows itself again to the willful decisions that direct personal activity. The first step is a vague, inarticulate wonder about origins. Hidden in that wonder is wonder about the mystery of existence, and particularly of human existence; that is the second step. Now human existence has many aspects, some of which can be thought of as higher or more truly human than others. The contention for which Farrer will "fight to the last ditch" is that there is an *interior* ladder: "active existence is thought of by us, and rightly thought of, as having levels of elevation and degrees of richness."[20] Our only direct experience of real creativity is the experience of the highest level of our conscious activity, the level of conscience and responsibility, of willing, deliberating, deciding, or choosing. For it is only in our voluntary acts that we make anything to be or not to be. A decision is something we create, and through our decisions we make ourselves.

The third stage of ascent is thus wonder about the mystery of freewill, and it is at this level that wonder about the creation becomes wonder about the Creator. Farrer's long defense of voluntarism in *The Freedom of the Will* is in fact a preliminary argument. His concern with human creativity leads to theological questions. If it be granted that the human will is free, is there such a creative power beneath everything, and not just the things *we* make to be? Is our own creative power underived, or does it spring from a deeper source of Will?[21]

Before these questions can be answered, however, there is an objection to be met. It is not a new one, but a more sophisticated version of the argument from brute facticity. Even if Farrer is right, and the will is free, it is quite as damaging to his case for theism to say that freewill is brute fact as it is to say the world as a whole is brute fact. And certain existentialist philosophers say just that; Sartre, for instance, would agree that human action is free, but he would deny that such freedom is a clue to the divine. On the contrary, according to this philosophy, our human freedom amounts to being handed, like it or not, the daunting assignment of working out an existence that is anyhow meaningless. It is the height of ridiculous irrationality, the most absurd of brute facts. To this idea Farrer's rebuttal is worth quoting:

> 'Now, my child,' they used to say to me, marking the end of a penal silence, 'Now you can say what you like.' My young lips were struck dumb by so portentous an option; and so it is, when existentialism throws my life into my lap, and says, 'Be yourself, my boy, and make it up as you go along.' The effect is like a paralytic stroke. I come to again, however, at last, and begin to remember — with what consolation to remember — my responsibilities.[22]

A previous paragraph mentioned the limitedness of our voluntary activity, in that we must always choose one act rather than another. Here Farrer makes the further point that because it *matters* which way we choose, there is yet another sense in which voluntary activity is limited. Besides being limited by what I cannot do, and by the mutual exclusivity of my choices, I am even further restrained in my actions by what I am *called* to do. There are limitations to free human choice which are neither physical nor temporal, but moral. I *cannot* walk through the wall and I *cannot* re-live yesterday; further, there are actions that I *must not* perform and others which I *must*, if I am aware of my responsibilities. Farrer argues that every serious person is aware of being "called" to certain actions, and since it is through our actions that we exist, our existence is limited by what we feel called upon to do and to refrain from doing. Responsibility is not an absolute limitation, for we can override it, but it is none the less real. Through its demands the actions by which each of us attains his or her being are called for. Everyone is called to become himself or herself.

To put it another way, our personal existence, our "selfhood," is not an object but an objective; not a possession but a goal. It is a highly flexible goal, but that does not mean we make it up as we go along. Rather, we discover the selfhood we are to attain in a lifetime of response to the claims made upon us by our environment. Freewill is not brute fact, since in exercising it no one acts in a vacuum. We cannot make ourselves in splendid isolation, oblivious to our interaction with other beings. Our freedom is absurd only if it is freedom-in-the-abstract, and this is just what Farrer denies by insisting that the responsibilities we experience in our interaction are real. Our choices are free, for they are not determined by our past; they are nevertheless called for.

In other beings we experience a "claimingness." But we cannot respond to all of the claims, and so it becomes necessary to evaluate our actions, and the necessity of valuation raises the question of God. Farrer admits that anyone "who approaches religion through moral thinking finds his feet on the beaten track to a mare's nest,"[23] and no doubt it is hard to make any judgment of value with which everyone will agree. Is it not, however, at least clear that the reality with the greatest claimingness on our regard, our valuation, and our action is human reality? This is the point from which Farrer proceeds. It is not a concept of humanity, he notes, that demands to be valued. "Humanity" or "rational agency" cannot awaken my regard or call for my decisions on their behalf, though Patrick or Patricia may do so. It is the actual presence — physical and spiritual — of our neighbors that makes moral thinking necessary. How are we to regard them?

That is a complex question and, according to Farrer, a theological question. He maintains that the "direct impact of the divine will is to be found, if anywhere, in the platitudinous region of basic valuation,"[24] and most clearly in our own valuation of other human beings. Farrer proposes that our neighbors lay claims upon us that limit our activity by requiring that we act towards them appropriately, and he proposes further that through the claims of our neighbors we encounter the claims of God. They are not two different claims, but a single call for action. This connection, however, is not an obvious one, and Farrer accordingly proposes to show how moral decision implies belief in God. How I regard any other being depends on what I suppose it is. At an obvious level, I shall respond differently to the figure in the corner according as I take it to be a waxwork or my cousin.

Less facetiously, Farrer argues that how I regard a cousin, or indeed any neighbor, depends on whether I take that neighbor to be a creature of God. Do I value my neighbors because their actions are harmonious with my own, because they will further my own purposes? Or do I carry my regard for others to the point of loving them as myself? It depends on whether I have grasped what my neighbors really are, and so the problem of contemplation *versus* manipulation remains an essential part of Farrer's argument, even when it is carried from the physical to the moral level. This is how he puts the question in one of his sermons:

how can you or I practically doubt that what commands our conscience in the last resort is the true Mary, or the true John, somewhere buried in the being of an actual Mary who, though so dear, is so naughty; or an actual John who, though his death would darken my day, is no influence for good in my life? Will you tell me that the true Mary, or the true John, is just an idea in my head? I cannot disprove you, but neither can I believe you. I ought to be ready to die for the true Mary, or the true John, and . . . if I were brave enough to die for my own *notion* of my neighbour's destiny, it would be nothing but colossal arrogance.[25]

It is not, however, colossal arrogance if "the true Mary or the true John" is instead the person whom God is making. The claim a neighbor makes on my regard, Farrer would say, is neither just the neighbor nor just my conscience. It is the claim or demand or will of God. What claims my respect is the essence of another person, the true self that God is at this moment bringing into existence. Believers "reverence not a single, but a double object, God in their neighbour, and their neighbour in God."[26] They experience their own being, and their neighbors' being, and are aware that the relation by which their existence is tied to their neighbors' is given to them and laid upon them by a Will sovereignly good. It is through every person with whom we have to do that our free action is limited or evoked, and the source of the limitation or evocation is a power who is actually creating and redeeming us along with our neighbors. Through interaction with other men and women, we become aware of God's will as a blueprint, a pattern that we can freely actualize or freely spurn.

The gist of Farrer's argument is this. In our own voluntary action we are acquainted with a natural creativity that is both free and finite. The acts in and through which we make ourselves, in response to moral claims, are free in that they are not determined "from below": they cannot be explained by our physical organism or our subconscious needs. These acts are finite in that they are directed or impinged upon "from above," by God. "If the highest, most voluntary part of human behaviour is not the act of God, then nowhere in the universe do we directly meet the divine love."[27] When we experience the "persuasive pressure" on our action that meets us through the claimingness of our neighbors, we experience ourselves entering a new creation through the double agency of our own will and the will of God. Our self-making is thus our being made.

That God is Creator does not mean that he made us in the past, nor does it mean that we are mere puppets. It means that "God makes his creatures make themselves . . . their action is their existence, and if they did not act of themselves, they would not exist in themselves — in fact, God would have failed after all to create them."[28] Our own finite existence is thus the hinge of the argument, but it is also the clue to all existence. Farrer's case for theism begins from ourself, or our neighbor, as the most informative instance, and extrapolates from this most directly-known case to those that are less immediate. From human finitude alone can the creatureliness of all other things be conjectured; what applies to human being applies to being in general. If God makes *us* make ourselves, he makes all that is, because our own active existence is neither isolated nor disembodied. We interact not only with our neighbors but with our physical environment. "To make you or me," Farrer puts it, "God must make half a universe."[29]

It was stated at the outset that to think about God is to think about his creative activity, and now at the end of this sketch of Farrer's approach to rational theology this point can be made clearer. In order to think about divine activity, we must have some contact with it, and it is that

contact which determines how we think. What we experience as "persuasive pressure" evoking our regard and
action can only be conceived as a personal will behind our
own. Further, it follows that our knowledge of God cannot
be any sort of detached examination, for we can only
know God if we are directly involved with him. This is just
what believers believe. "The will of God is everywhere present: it is experienced by being obeyed. When we make our
own will the prolongation of God's will for us and in us,
then we know God."[30]

Proof of God's existence, it has been said, is for Farrer
a kind of "testing." Is there any experiential evidence for
the existence of God the Creator? Farrer answers that there
is indeed "experimental proof," but that it can only be personal. It is not in the nature of the case that scientific objec-
tivity should be expected, and the theist must be tough
enough to assert that the act of religious obedience is our
privileged access to the knowledge of God. The only way
to test the assumption that God exists is to "will the will of
God."

This is one of Farrer's most characteristic phrases, and
it is more than a pious slogan. "Willing the will of God"
names a real experience. Nor is it so unimaginable a phrase
as it sounds at first. The activity of God's will living in our
own action can be defined by saying, "the more it is God,
the more it is I; and the more it is I, the more it is God."[31]
Certainly this is a paradoxical definition, yet there are
analogies in other activities. Runners, for example, main-
tain that there comes a moment in their running when it is
no longer they who are pounding the pavement, but the
pavement that is pounding them. They say that they are
not running, but being run. Musicians often speak of their
best performances in the same paradoxical way: "When I

am really singing at the top of my form the song sings itself." These are experiences where runners or musicians do something they did not have it in them to do. To that extent, there is an analogy to the experience which believers in God may describe by asserting the paradox that their best, most authentic thoughts and actions are not theirs at all. Action is most free when it carries out the blue-print, and most creative when it is least original.

Such paradoxes are tolerable only if there is no other way to express a real experience, and Farrer judges that it is "a paradox of language, but a commonplace of experience, that a man is never so truly himself as when his action is God's."[32] The paradigm is the experience of prayer. Even in his philosophical *Faith and Speculation* he singles out prayer as the most compelling evidence for God. It is not a move that most philosophers would make, yet Farrer insists that the philosopher who brushes away as "pious rant" all personal accounts of the experience of prayer might as well close the inquiry before it begins. If it be asked what the practical consequences of belief in God are, Farrer's own answer is that the believer's conviction that the Creator works by making his creatures make themselves is expressed through prayer. By praying we exercise our regard for the neighbors whom God is actually making and redeeming.

God's existence can only be tested personally, in a life that Farrer (with some reservations) calls an experiment in drawing upon First Causality. We can perform this experiment only upon ourselves. Yet no one's lifetime is long enough to try every conceivable way of cooperating with the will of God, and so we may extend the experiment by proxy, adding to our own the "experimental proof" of men and women whose lives are not only good but holy. There is indirect evidence, in other words, in the acts of those who, by exercising the highest human powers in the freest and most personal way, have themselves "willed the will of God." Farrer describes the saints as those who have "transmitted the causality of God, by adherence to him in the apex of their wills";[33] holy living touches the point of transition where divine action activates human action.

Farrer's ascent of the ladder of created being and Bonaventure's both culminate in the "apex of the will." Such proof of theism is obviously not an inescapable demonstration, and at every step of the way there will be those who become sceptical and refuse to travel further. This is not to say, however, that only an astute and sophisticated reasoner can make the whole journey. Farrer does think that the evidence of faith is necessarily "aristocratic," but by that he means that saints are rare, not that philosophers alone can be true theists. His axiom is that rational theology can only prolong a basic, theistic movement of thought which the simplest of minds can make, and which precedes philosophical reasoning.[34] At the same time, however, he has no desire to conceal the difficulties. It has never been easy to think about the relation of our godly action to God's action in us. To think about God strains to the uttermost the powers of the human mind. "How could it be otherwise," Farrer asks, "if God is God? In this act there is no rest . . . we have never arrived; as we seem on the point to do so, our thought evaporates . . . If we wish to think on, we must return humbly to the bottom of the ladder, and climb again."[35]

§5

In conclusion, four observations can be made about Farrer's journey into God. First, it needs to be repeated that Farrer regards theology and spirituality as essentially one. While they are not identical, each complements the other, and both come to rest in unrestricted Will. As his Cavalier-and-Roundhead parable suggests, Farrer disagrees with the suggestion often made that reasoning from the world to a divine Cause, and trusting religious experience, are separate paths to belief in God. His own position is that the practice of religion

> is what brings life to our reasonings about the world's ultimate Cause, and gives reality to them; while on the other side our reasonings about the world give sense and definition to a religious faith in God. It isn't a choice between following the reason and trusting the heart. It is a matter of putting heart into a rational conviction, *and* bringing mind into the heart's devotion.[36]

The second point is similar. Even Farrer's most forbiddingly philosophical arguments are always grounded in something that is prior to them. Their foundation lies in experiences believers recognize as the substance of their living-out of faith in God. All believers think about their faith in some fashion; while belief in God must certainly be lived as well as thought, without being thought it cannot be lived. Theology in this sense is not incidental, nor is it a parasite on the life of faith. It is one of religion's vital organs. "I do not know," Farrer declares, "what the difference between 'plain practical religion' and 'theology' is supposed to be."[37] How can a faith that is undefined and unexpressed be practical?

Every believer is to some extent a theologian. If, like Farrer, he or she has a philosophical turn of mind, the use of somewhat technical language may be the best and most convincing way to give meaning and order to faith. Farrer's own vocabulary — "freewill," "causality," "existence," "finitude," and so on — is appropriate only to the extent that it succeeds in giving precise and reasonable expression to a reality that is by no means merely academic. Philosophical theology can only refine and develop the theological language believers already use, above all the language in which they frame their worship. Farrer the preacher, for instance, alludes to the Collect for Peace from the Prayer Book office of matins in his statement that "the whole mystery of practical religion comes down to that familiar phrase of our daily prayer, 'whose service is perfect freedom.' "[38] It is precisely the same mystery of practical religion, the paradox of willing the will of God, that Farrer the theologian works to illuminate in *Faith and Speculation* and *The Freedom of the Will*.

A third observation is more general. Throughout his writing Farrer stresses what can only be called a contemplative attitude. When he speaks of contemplating natural mysteries as the starting-point of rational theology, however, he is not suggesting the advanced stages of mystical experience. Farrer calls himself the least mystical of men, and by contemplation he means an openness to wonder, a thirst for real being, a meditative curiosity. Where preoccupation with control is the prevailing attitude, as it is in our technological age, such curiosity is all too easily stifled. Insofar as we are concerned with what things can do for us, with manipulating them, it is unlikely that we shall even raise the question, "what *is* this?" And without asking that most fundamental of questions it is useless to try to think about God. We cannot control God, nor does God control us. He draws us through our own freewill. We know him best when we see our neighbors as they are; do we see them most truly, Farrer asks, "when we let ourselves love them, even poetize a bit about them, when we let our minds free to respond to them, or when we take them to pieces with analytical exactitude?"[39] On the answer hangs the further question of how seriously we are able to take the idea of God.

Personal interaction is the key for Farrer, but the key unlocks the whole creation. The God who makes things make themselves can be recognized everywhere, by anyone who is willing to wonder. G.K. Chesterton ends a poem with these lines:

And stones still shine along the road
That are and cannot be.[40]

The feeling that things "are and cannot be," that the world is not self-explanatory, gives force to the question "why is it so?" And that is the beginning of theistic theology, the first step of Jacob's ladder.

It should be said in closing that Farrer thinks rational theology to be important and, to some degree, necessary, but he never supposes that it is enough. It is useful to argue the reasonableness of theism by showing that the believer's view of the world is no scandal to philosophy and that, moreover, it is the only view that does justice to the whole range of human experience. But theism is "mere creator-worship," and it cannot stand alone. There comes a point when the theistic reasoner "looks at the world, and wonders why he ever dreamt of looking beyond it; why he ever supposed it to require a cause outside itself, an origin transcendent or divine."[41] There may be evidence for creative providence in the natural order, but there seems to be much evidence against it — the evidence of pain and evil. How is it possible to reconcile "love almighty and ills unlimited"? That is the title of one of Farrer's books, and he is acutely aware of the grave objection to theistic belief presented by physical pain, by moral evil, and also by sin. Though we aspire to will the will of God, we fail miserably. We recognize the blue-print, yet we build our lives to suit ourselves. Pain, evil, and sin make us "turn to God not as an explanatory cause, but as a saving power; not as the ground of all existence, but as a rock on which to plant our feet."[42]

God as he is known through his activity in nature is sovereign Will, but God as Christians know him through his supernatural revelation is more. It is artificial to separate natural knowledge of God from the truth he discloses about himself, especially when discussing a theologian whose thought thoroughly integrates the two. There are no pure theists among the adherents of any religion, and Farrer's is above all a deeply Christian theism. Rational theology cannot answer the question of salvation, for that answer is given by God who in Christ reconciles us to himself. *To the One God, therefore, who wonderfully creates and yet more wonderfully restores the dignity of human nature, Father, Son and Holy Spirit, be ascribed as is most justly due all might, majesty, dominion and power, henceforth and forever.*

II

POETRY AND THE GOSPEL OF MARK

And as they came down from the mountain, he charged them that they should tell no man what things they had seen, till the Son of Man were risen from the dead. And they kept that saying with themselves, questioning one with another what the rising from the dead should mean. ST MARK, IX, 9-10

JACOB IN HIS DREAM saw a ladder on which angels were both ascending and descending. If from one point of view theology can be seen as the ascent of the heart and mind to God, from another it is the reception of the revelation brought by Christ when, for us and for our salvation, he came down from heaven. The image that gives these lectures their title might suggest that natural or rational theology simply climbs as far as is humanly possible, and is met halfway up the ladder by supernaturally revealed answers to its most difficult questions. Using the metaphor of motion in two directions in this way, however, distorts Farrer's much subtler understanding of how natural theology and revealed theology are related.

If we speak of an upward and a downward component, one human and the other divine, both are present whenever anyone thinks theologically, either about God's action in making things make themselves, or about his supernatural action in Christ. Rational theology starts from creation, yet Farrer considers God's creativity itself as "a coming down from heaven, an indwelling of his creatures,"[1] including the human creatures whose minds aspire to think theistically. On the other hand, revealed theology starts from God's supernatural acts, but these too are exercised in and through finite creatures; more specifically, through human minds that recognize and accept certain events as God's self-disclosures. There is a human factor in revelation, the cooperation of those who ponder and interpret God's supernatural action.

Shall we say that God acts generally through nature, but specifically in revelation? That is somewhat closer to Farrer's position, but it is still too simple. As the last lecture suggested, God's creativity is everywhere present, but it is recognized particularly in his making men and women make themselves. Only after that is it affirmed of every other finite being. What is glimpsed through the dark glass of voluntary action and freewill is a sovereign power which, the believer can only conclude, must extend to all that is.

The same movement from particular to general can be seen from a historical standpoint. It is a relatively late and sophisticated development of religious thought which sees God as the Will that holds absolutely everything in being. It was only centuries after his ancestors had experienced God's saving power at the Red Sea that the psalmist could sing that "the earth is the Lord's and the fulness thereof" (Ps. 24:1). Later still is the first chapter of Genesis, which casts into narrative form the same conviction that the God of Israel is the God by whose voluntary act all things exist.

Farrer's treatment of these two Old Testament stories, the tale of creation and the account of the exodus from Egypt, is especially instructive *apropos* his understanding of natural and revealed knowledge of God. Both narratives are part of the scripture that Christians take to be the embodiment of God's revealed word. Farrer suggests, however, that both are also products of the kind of thinking discussed in the last lecture under the rubric of natural theology. The creation story, he notes, gives the impression that its author "had an inquiring mind and a strong curiosity about the origins of things"; he was moved to write "in vivid figures what he saw by faith of God's shaping power, the power which shapes things, and above all, men, here and now."[2] In his own way and using his own symbolic idiom, this unknown Israelite was setting down a kind of natural theology.

Israel's escape from Pharoah's army is more particular and is, in fact, the central miracle of the Old Testament. But it is not fundamentally different. What, Farrer asks, happened at the Red Sea?

> A stray hot wind, blowing all night, pushed the shallow water off the sands of Suez. The Israelites slipped across under cover of dark. The Egyptian chariotry followed at the crack of dawn, their wheels stuck in the sand and the water came back on them. Only Moses was inspired to will with the will of God and to lead Israel over.[3]

This, the chief among God's mighty acts, had a human component. There was a recognition of divine purpose and a cooperation with it that Farrer describes in the phrase that is the theme of his philosophical theology: Moses "willed the will of God."

Farrer is no rationalizer; his purpose is not to explain away the Old Testament stories but to understand them. His point is that whatever revelation may be, it is not a one-sided affair. No miracle, even the crossing of the Red Sea, is purely God's act. The physical event, the wind and the water, had to be interpreted as expressing divine purpose, a purpose that demanded cooperation. Both were the human contribution of an individual "inspired to will with the will of God." This is not to say that Farrer simply conflates the human and divine aspects of the revelatory process. God's supernatural grace is not identical with human will and discernment. If it were, why talk about God? To suppose that God is the back side of human nature is not theism, but pantheism, and Christianity cannot in Farrer's estimation survive without a distinction between natural reason and supernatural revelation.

Up to this point all that has been said is that reason and revelation are not utterly different, nor are they identical. What, then, can be said about them? The scholastic formula for the relationship was *gratia perficit naturam, non tollit*. Farrer offers a gloss on this venerable tag, proposing that "the supernatural enhances and intensifies, but does not remove nature."[4] God's acts in revelation are not discontinuous with his acts through nature, and the human act of understanding what is revealed is not discontinuous with the mental action that understands natural existence as the work of God. Farrer's special interest is in the human contribution. How, he asks, does God "enhance" natural reasoning, enabling human minds to appropriate the truth he reveals about himself?

One indication of the direction his answer takes can be found in Farrer's interpretations, just mentioned, of the creation and exodus stories. The author of Genesis 1 wrote "in vivid figures," and Moses was "inspired." Farrer's twin keys to understanding revelation's supernatural enhancement or intensification of human intelligence are *images* and *inspiration*. Revealed truth does not lie in propositions or sentences or concepts, but in images that are related, compared, and interwoven by inspired imagination. Inspiration is supernaturalized thinking that works at the divine riddle reflected in a glass of images.

Farrer does not, however, concoct this definition out of nowhere. He almost never discusses revelation in the abstract, for "revelation in general" is very nearly a contradiction in terms. His actual starting-point is a lifelong study of the scriptures that Christians already accept as revelation *par excellence,* revelation as such, without qualification. Images and inspiration are the factors he discerns in the thought of those who wrote what he takes as his standard of revealed truth, the canonical books of the Old and New Testaments. We cannot decide in advance how God ought to reveal himself and then look about to see whether he has done it, concluding perhaps that there is quite a lot of revelation in the Bible. Farrer's procedure is just the reverse. He does not bend his reading of scripture to fit a notion of God's self-communication; he draws his understanding of revelation from scripture.

It should be pointed out that natural theology also starts from a standard example although, as the last lecture showed, it is not so easy to decide which example to use. We cannot speak of all existence as dependent on God before we know what we are talking about, and so Farrer's argument focuses on one instance of createdness that he regards as the clearest — our own. This is an active existence in which two agents, divine and human, are at work. Similarly, we cannot speak of revelation without having a standard example in mind. Christianity believes its scriptures to be the revealed word of God, and while it may well be that other faiths have something of revelation in them, Farrer prefers to limit himself to what he accepts as *the* revelation of God.[5]

God "shows us his face in the scriptural glass," provided we make proper use of it. As in the case of knowledge of God through creation, a contemplative attitude is the first prerequisite; read as an almanac of information, the scriptures quickly become opaque. Farrer's own approach, evident in his sermons and especially in devotional works like *The Triple Victory,* is to read with the care and concentration that should be given to poetry. To "inwardly digest" scripture is a process not unlike ruminating on a poem, mulling it over and savoring the words as well as taking it in great sweeps. But Farrer turns poetic reflection on scripture to scholarly as well as to devotional purposes. "Scripture and metaphysics," he writes, "are equally my study, and poetry is my pleasure."[6] Poetic imagination, he urges, offers useful and illuminating comparisons to inspiration in the theological sense. The relationship between scripture and poetry, then, is the topic of this lecture, although it will be seen that metaphysics also insists on making itself heard in Farrer's account of inspiration.

The rather abstract remarks of this introductory section can be summed up as follows. Revelation, according to Christian belief, bestows knowledge of God that natural theology cannot achieve. It surpasses rational thinking about God, not by adding to it, but by enhancing or intensifying it through a process that can be studied in the Christian scriptures, which are Farrer's standard of revealed truth. In the New Testament, he writes, "we can as it were overhear men doing supernatural thinking of a privileged order, with pens in their hands."[7] What is overheard is inspired thinking. It expresses itself through images and unfolds in a way that Farrer understands by comparing it with poetic imagination. His treatment of revealed theology is thus rooted in New Testament studies, and those studies are nourished by his keen sensitivity to the mode and matter of poetry.

§2

"But please don't think," Farrer warns, "that I am going to tell you that theology is just figurative poetry: that is a very wicked thing to say, though some people have not shrunk from it."[8] Theology prolongs a more basic religious language, and religious language resembles poetry in form though not necessarily in content. A particular subject matter, the relation of humanity to God, makes such language religious; its use of images to convey that relation makes it poetic. "There is only one practical relation of the human person to the divine," Farrer insists, "and that is the voluntary relation of which faith, obedience, love and their contraries are the modalities."[9] The theologian who is inclined to philosophy may say that God is Pure Act or Unconditioned Will, but the religious affirmation that lies behind such technical phrases is more immediately expressed when the psalmist declares that "the Lord is king!"

Theology will strive for the greatest possible precision in defining that relationship, but long before there were philosophical theologians, believers voiced their faith in God through images, parables, figures, and stories. The tradition of ancient Israel saw God as a rock of salvation, a fortress and a shield. The Old Testament also describes God in images and parables drawn from particular aspects of human life which themselves bear some resemblance to divine power. God is seen as the cause and exemplar of crucial activities that bring order to family and society; he is the "divine archetype of a tribal patriarch, the warrior-champion of his people, a stern disciplinarian, a benevolent provider, a wise leader."[10] God is also likened to a shepherd, a comforting mother and, most frequently, a king.

Farrer would stress that these are not primarily concepts, but images. Behind the symbolism of God as king is not an idea of royalty but something more concrete — the actual human king at Jerusalem. When human kings arose in Israel, an invisible divine king stood behind their throne. "Indeed, kingship worthy of the name," Farrer writes, "is distinguished from mere leadership by the divinity which supports it."[11] How the divine archetype and the earthly image are related is a complex question. The relationship is expressed in the image itself, and what it consists in cannot be stated in a few precise words. David the king is certainly not the same as the Lord of Hosts, yet Farrer claims for them an identity of action such that David's acts embody and reveal God's purposes. His victories are the work of God, and through him the heavenly king rules Israel.

Farrer thinks it a wise saying that "in Scripture there is not a line of theology, and of philosophy not so much as an echo."[12] He does not suppose that any of the Old Testament authors, scribes, annotators and revisers operated by means of a neat and consistent theory of how their human symbols referred to the divine. It is enough that King David is recognized as a visible image of deity. Such symbolism follows an imaginative logic of its own in which connotations and layers of meaning function poetically, defying systematization. It can be observed only by tracing how, for example, the image of kingship developed.

The association of image and archetype, human kingship and divine sovereignty, was a close one from earliest times. Sometimes it verged on idolatry, for graven images are not the only ones that can become idols through being mistaken for the invisible reality in which they participate. So long as the distinction was kept, the human instrument could properly symbolize the divine will that wielded it. "Of Jehovah the King, King David is the instrument; then David's righteous acts are as the acts of God."[13] But not all of David's acts were righteous, as Nathan the prophet so scathingly pointed out to him in reference to his conduct with Bathsheba. In the long run David's kingdom was an inadequate symbol, for it failed to embody the holiness and power of Israel's God. When the earthly embodiment of the archetype of kingship came to an end as Israel and Judah ceased to be political monarchies, this failure was seen as the withdrawal of divine favor from human kingship.

The image of kingship, however, was not abolished. Though there was no longer a human reflection of divine majesty, no viceregent of the Lord, that image lived on. God was still king, and Israel came to see that David's kingdom had been only the foreshadowing of a holy and universal kingdom in which the sovereignty of God would be adequately manifested. As David had received God's anointing at the hands of Samuel, so there would be a new Anointed. A Messiah, a greater David, would reign. After the exile, Israel's hopes continued to be shaped and expressed by the image of the kingdom of God. What the image meant, who the king would be, how the kingdom would enter the world, and what its relation would be to the power of the nations were questions expounded in further images, such as those of the book of Daniel and, later still, in apocalyptic writings like the book of Enoch.

The messianic hopes that clustered about the image of the kingdom of God were fulfilled, as Farrer puts it, only when the image itself was "reborn" in the thoughts and words and deeds of Jesus of Nazareth. Not only the image of kingship but also many others underwent a decisive transformation. The birth of Christianity, in his memorable phrase, was a "rebirth of images," the images of Israel set out in what Christians now call the Old Testament. Before considering how Farrer develops this thesis, however, something more must be said about the poetic role which, in his view, images play in religious thinking.

"The human imagination," Farrer writes in his earliest biblical study, "has always been controlled by certain basic images, in which man's own nature, his relation to his fellows, and his dependence upon the divine power find expression."[14] It is no coincidence that all three of these themes appeared in the last lecture. Finite human selfhood, both creative and created, the regard claimed by neighbors, and dependence upon an unrestricted Will that shapes all — these for Farrer are the elements of theistic philosophy, the reasoned exposition of obedient interaction with divine Will.

Images, especially visual and narrative images, are inseparable from religious experience. The bare notion of divine power has no place in the language of worship, because this notion is unimaginable. Only a suitable image can move the heart, by presenting the reality for which it stands. Farrer rejects as "exceedingly stupid" the idea that exact prose states reality, while symbols merely evoke emotion. Images, he agrees, do engage feelings, but they do so because they also confront us with the manysidedness of real being. Precise, scientific prose, on the contrary, always involves abstraction from — and impoverishment of — its object.

Some images are so widespread as to be almost a universal language, and so old that their origins are lost in the past. "Who first saw life as a springing fountain, or guilt as dirt needing to be purged away?"[15] No one knows or ever will, but those images have entered the vocabulary common to poets and sages in many times and places. Such basic images are not static, however; the development of one image in one religious and cultural tradition, the image of kingship in Israel, has been mentioned above. As imagination carries their meaning forward, images are compared, merged, contrasted and interrelated. Nor is the process dead today. We need only recall how an image as old as Noah's ark, the dove, was revived not many years ago, with the hawk as its counterpole.

Theology itself is in part a refinement of imagery, in that it distinguishes and brings order to the multiple levels of meaning conveyed by images of human interaction with God. The most that rational theology can achieve is a refined way of speaking analogically about God, and what are analogies, Farrer asks in *The Glass of Vision*, but sober and criticized images? He does not suppose that their sobriety brings theological analogies closer to the truth than the images they refine. It is as refreshing as it is unusual to find so erudite a theologian as Farrer allowing that "if you like to say that all theologies are dead idolatries of the mind, well, in a sense, so they are."[16] Especially in the study of scripture, it is impossible to get behind the images and find an imageless truth. Theology can suggest how living images should be read; it cannot replace them.

The use of images is the counterpart to that almost reverent willingness to contemplate real being which Farrer counts as the indispensable prerequisite to any awareness of God. Poets, rather than scientists, may be best equipped to express such an attitude of respect for what things really are — although a scientist may also be a poet. Precise prose serves admirably to analyze things, but poetry is a means of describing them. Farrer elaborates this point by contrasting two meanings of the question, "what is this?" An analytical approach will give one answer; a descriptive approach, quite another. "As grammarians may break up sentences into words and words into letters, so the scientist analyzes the world into the factors which in his view compose it."[17] To answer analytically the question, "what is this?" is to show the arrangement of its parts.

The same question, however, takes on quite a different nuance when by asking "what is this?" we want to know "what is it *like*; what is its individual character?" This second meaning of the question requires that we use our words to describe the qualities things have, by comparing them with other things. "All the world's a stage" makes such a comparison by means of a metaphor. There is nothing remarkable about metaphors as such, and it is hard to utter three consecutive sentences without using at least one. But to use words well in this way depends on a gift for grasping new and profound resemblances; a person with this gift can illuminate the nature of things by combining images metaphorically.

This ability to see and express deep resemblances is poetic insight. Poets experience new realities, and they experience familiar things more thoroughly. They *see* in a fresh and revealing way and, when their poetry is successful, they allow their readers to share something of their own intense perception. Dorothy Sayers, herself a considerable poet, has put this aspect of poetic communication well: "We did not know it before, but the moment the poet has shown it to us, we know that somehow or other, we had always really known it."[18]

What is it that poetry brings to our attention? There is hardly a subject to which poets have not turned their pens, so the answer might be, "anything at all." Still, there is more likely to be a useful parallel to theology in great and serious poetry than in nursery rhymes, even though Farrer wrily observes that in " 'Sing a Song of Sixpence' we might claim to be dealing with the eternal essence of poetry, for this sort of thing has been going on since men and black-birds first began to sing."[19] There is plenty of poetry about everyday things, but poets can also unveil what is under the surface of the commonplace and bring into focus im-portant truths that do not fit into our customary categories.

There is a further point about the use of metaphor that is even more important. The more unique the thing to be described, the harder it is to find adequate comparisons. When single metaphors no longer do the descriptive job, one comparison has to be qualified and corrected by another. Here is an example of this combination of images: "the moon was a ghostly galleon." The poet has taken a single metaphor, the moon as a galleon, and qualified it by the addition of another. The conjunction of "ghost" and "galleon," Farrer would suggest, poses a riddle. We are in-vited to take the associations of "ghost" (an awesome, shadowy figure shrouded in white, appearing by night in lonely places), and to balance them with the associations of "galleon" (a bulky, antique vessel, floating on the high sea, driven by the wind). Where those two sets of associa-tions intersect, we have the right effect: that is what the moon was *like*.

To dissect the poet's riddle in this way is just the op-posite of poetry, and no analysis can replace the immediate effect of juxtaposing "ghost" and "galleon." For each of these images the list of connotations and overtones could be lengthened almost indefinitely, but the result would be no closer to the meaning of their combination. There is, in fact, no meaning that can be stated in other words. The combination either works or it does not; its effect is not intellectual but, primarily, imaginative. What the poet "means" is what he means to *do*, and that is to spark an imaginative insight in those who read the poem. Moreover there is no external logical intersection involved, for "ghost" and "galleon" do not overlap in the way that "parent" and "woman" do to produce "mother." The intersection that solves the riddle is something that is neither a ghost nor a galleon, but simply itself — the moon, seen in a fresh way. It is not just the poet's emotional reaction to the moon, but the way it really is.

This lunar excursion is not irrelevant to theology. If the moon, which is not inherently metaphysical or mysterious, merits a poetic description that on examination can be seen to involve a complex act of imagination, what of a truly unique reality? How can the soul, for example, be described? The last lecture showed how Farrer's rational theology takes its bearings from the highest level of human activity, the "apex of the will" that focuses our finite creativity. Even in this relatively straightforward description metaphor still lurks. "Apex" is an image borrowed from geometry, as "focus" is from optics, to say nothing of the variety of qualities suggested by "creativity." The point, however, is not to stalk metaphors but to ask how we can locate the elusive reality on which they converge. By way of answer, Farrer poses a more picturesque riddle. What must be found is

> not the emotion, but the real being which is like a flame, a dynamo, a weighing-scale and an illumination, and which is also the centre of your own existence. I reply: 'That is easy. It is what I have and what I am.' But the riddle is not a mere riddle: by suggesting both contrast and likeness it gives us a vivid perception of what the soul is.[20]

We cannot speak properly or logically about the soul, but only *ana*logically, in images and metaphors. Does that mean it does not exist? Only to those who are obsessed with analytic precision. The soul is unique. It is like nothing else, and so it fits no category.

If we insist on clarity and distinctness as the criterion of all our serious thinking, the course of our decisions about what is real and what is not will be like the frantic sledge ride in the Russian story. Nothing must be spared in holding off the wolf pack that pursues the flight of the prince, and so "one after another of the sledge-team is thrown to the following wolves: knowledge of body, knowledge of soul, knowledge of knowledge in turn glut the jaws of darkness." And who is it, Farrer asks, that must be preserved, whatever the cost, to the end of the journey? The prince is a principle, the ideal of analytical precision, the criterion "exclusive of all mystery, of everything that is baffling."[21] Knowledge of selfhood cannot be precise because the soul is unique.

Yet however unique my own selfhood is, God is even more unique; "uniquely unique," as a Frenchman once said to Farrer. I am not all the selfhood there is, for my neighbors are living souls too; but God, as the scholastics often pointed out, is all the deity there is. Descriptions of God baffle us even more than descriptions of the soul. The only recourse is metaphor. Nevertheless Farrer, alluding to a favorite text, does not think it a scandal that we know God only "through a glass and *in a riddle*." Statements about God, however refined, are riddling similitudes. "Let us call him the *eternal spirit*. That is as much to say, 'Find a being in whom the living act of personality and the changelessness of mathematical truth meet and coincide.' "[22]

It has been suggested that in order to understand revelation Farrer proposes to overhear inspired thinking as it takes place. This second section began by marking some of the developments of a single Old Testament image, "king," and concluded with a general account of the comparisons Farrer draws between the poetic and theological uses of metaphor. These threads must now be drawn together and brought to bear on his interpretation of the New Testament, especially of the Gospel of Mark.

§3

The New Testament books were written by poets. In somewhat exaggerated form, this is the leading idea of Farrer's full-length biblical studies. He devotes much of his attention to the way these authors recombine, compare, rearrange and contrast the imagery inherited from Israel's long tradition. In other words, there is a close resemblance between the poetic use of metaphor and the inspired use of images. Convinced that the inspiration of scripture is poetic as well as divine, Farrer suggests that the way literary critics interpret poetry can usefully be applied to the New Testament. There are differences, of course, because none of the New Testament books is pure poetry. In any case, "St Mark's Gospel (let us say) is neither a poem nor a play, and it has to be interpreted as what it is, not as what it is not."[23] The criticism of poetry is only an analogy, but it may be a fruitful analogy.

Nothing could be more different than Farrer's literary or poetic approach to the Gospel of Mark from the reigning form-criticism of his day. His own concern is with St Mark's book, his inspired thinking as a whole. As Farrer sees it, his task is to observe the evangelist's thinking "from inside, to *become*, as far as that is possible, St Mark in the act of gospel-writing."[24] By rethinking his thoughts, Farrer hopes to follow the actual course of St Mark's inspired imagination at work.

More than old-fashioned piety is expressed in Farrer's consistent use of "St Mark" for the author of the earliest gospel. The title reflects his conviction that St Mark was no anonymous scribe but a genuine author whose aims, beliefs and attitudes are expressed in what he writes. It is on this point in particular that Farrer felt bound to part company with many of the form-critics. Their general theory in regard to the Gospel of Mark was that the book as we have it is essentially a patchwork. The pieces, especially in the first eight chapters, are paragraphs which the evangelist simply copied, or wrote down as he heard them, and then somewhat clumsily stitched together. Because it regarded the evangelist as having contributed nothing but the seams, this phase of form-criticism concerned itself with the patches. Farrer, changing the metaphor, writes that this approach to the Gospel of Mark "hopes by stripping down to obtain nuggets of solid ore, the true metal of primitive tradition."[25] Excising the easily spotted editorial connections, it was thought, allows the paragraphs of older narrative to be recovered intact. Farrer was dissatisfied with an approach that in his view reduces the earliest gospel to "paragraphs plus a self-betraying editorial hand." When it is taken to extremes, he notes with some dismay, the result is that

> our oldest and best narrative authority is treated as individually negligible, a piecer together of traditions, a hack editor. We make haste to shoulder him out of the way, that we may lay our hands upon an impersonal and disjointed mass of tradition, which he is supposed to have had in his desk, or in his memory. We pull the Marcan mosaic to bits, and then it is amazing how free we find ourselves to reconstruct the ikon of Christ according to enlightened principles.[26]

To treat St Mark as negligible begs an important question, that of St Mark's purpose in writing his book. How can it be decided in advance, Farrer wants to know, what the evangelist "must have been" doing? Why should it

simply be assumed that he was interested only in pre-
serving, more or less unchanged, the paragraphs and anecdotes that were circulating at the time? How can we be sure
that St Mark did not adapt his materials to some larger
purpose of his own? To presuppose that he had no larger
design in mind is to decide in advance what sort of book
the earliest gospel is; would it not therefore be more sensi-
ble to examine the book itself, and try to discern on the
basis of that evidence — the only evidence, after all, that
we have — what in fact St Mark *was* doing?

Farrer's quarrel with form-criticism ought not to be
exaggerated. He was very much interested in distinguish-
ing St Mark's own contribution to the gospel that bears his
name from the traditional material from which he worked.
Farrer insists, however, that this is not a distinction of
truth but of time. Unless divine inspiration is ruled out
from the start, what Christ did and said in Galilee and
what the evangelist wrote years later as commentary and
interpretation are both aspects of revelation. Of the combination of factual tradition with the interpreter-Spirit, not
only in St Mark's book but throughout the New Testament, Farrer says briefly, "this *was* Christianity."[27]

In the long run, the justice of Farrer's negative ap-
praisal of one school of New Testament exegesis is much
less important that his own positive contribution. It is a
contribution not only to the academic study of the Christian scripture, but to the spiritual use of the Bible as well.
"Liberal enlightenment," he writes, "claims to have opened
the scriptural casket, but there appears now to be nothing
inside — nothing, anyhow, which ordinary people feel
moved to seek through the forbidding discipline of spiritual reading."[28] The last section will have more to say on this
topic. First, however, what does Farrer mean by claiming
that St Mark was not a compiler but an author?

As opposed to an editor or a copyist, the author of a book writes everything with an eye to some overall purpose and plan. The working-out of a large compositional pattern, Farrer argues, necessarily influences each of its many smaller patterns — sentences, paragraphs, chapters — so that the unity of the whole work takes priority over its constituent parts. Besides being subordinated to the whole, every sentence after the first will also bear some relation to what has gone before. An author who writes with no regard to what has already been written can scarcely be called an author. That may be how to write an anthology; it is not the way books are written. The earlier parts of a unified piece of writing bear suggestions that later developments will carry forward, while later parts echo what has gone before.

Farrer is thus quite willing to agree that in St Mark's book, "the paragraphs are mostly self-contained. They are strung together like beads on a string. But perhaps," he continues, "they are strung with art; perhaps each bead is carved by the jeweller for the place it is to occupy in the row."[29] The individual paragraphs, that is to say, may have intelligible sequence as parts of an overall design, and an inner form that likewise reflects the whole book's purpose. These are the ideas that Farrer sets out to test in two full-length studies of the earliest gospel, numerous essays, and a third book left unfinished at his death.

The pattern to which St Mark adapts his paragraphs is not, however, a logical pattern like the sequence of steps in a geometrical construction; nor is it primarily a chronological pattern like the sequence of episodes in a historical narrative. It is, rather, a symbolic and theological pattern. "The most primitive of the Evangelists," as Farrer remarks, "cannot narrate the story of Christ without coming under the constraint of the Spirit, obliging him to set forth the image of Christ as what the Spirit now shows it essentially to have been, rather than as what it could have been seen at the time to be."[30] It is not that St Mark dreamed up his historical account, but only that he supplied its narrative form, a form that shows his interest in more than just chronological order.

St Mark's book is an "ikon of Christ," a complex and somewhat formal patterning of traditions interwoven with material drawn from that matrix of religious images, the scriptures of Israel. This is a third factor in St Mark's thinking. He writes with constant reference to his overall purpose, to what he has already written, and to the knowledge of God's ways expressed in the Old Testament's imagery. All of these factors make the evangelist's way of writing more like literary and poetic technique than anything else. As its images and their relations unfold, the earliest of the gospels develops a rhythm of its own. Its "formal recurrences are St Mark's poetical magic: one paragraph subtly echoes another, emphasizing persistent themes and throwing variations into relief."[31] St Mark is a jeweler who carves his beads as he strings them.

Can the idea that St Mark was an author writing in so complex a manner as this seriously be entertained? It would be much more difficult if there were no independent evidence that the imagination of first century Christians ran along such lines. But according to Farrer there is evidence, the evidence of the Revelation of St John the Divine, which he calls "the one great poem which the first Christian age produced." Here is a unified web of imaginative association, in which the imagery of the books of Daniel and Ezekiel is combined with the expectation of Christ's imminent return in glory to give a highly detailed pattern revolving around the symbolism of the number seven. The Apocalypse is "one great structure of divination in which numbered sets of things are 'squared' with one another"[32] — seven letters to the churches of Asia, seven seals broken to release visions of the end, seven trumpets heralding further visions. The kind of poetic intersection illustrated above in the simple phrase "ghostly galleon" occurs countless times as St John weaves his strands of allusion.

No doubt the Apocalypse is an extreme case. Even so, Farrer considers that an extreme example is useful in overthrowing a universal negative, such as the judgment that poetic imagination is not to be found in early Christian thought. If St John could seek and find inspiration through meditating on the great images of the Old Testament in light of the Christian message, then it is all the more likely that other Christian writers of the first age received inspiration through such means.

So thoroughly does a quasi-poetic movement of images imbue the writings of the early church that Farrer sees the birth of Christianity as equivalent to a rebirth of images. He connects it with the Spirit poured out at Pentecost, the fruits of which included prophecy as well as ecstatic utterance; and by prophecy the primitive church understood preaching that was not just exhortation, but a development and application of what had already been said in the scriptures.

It was Jesus himself, moreover, who initiated the rebirth of images. In Christ's existence were fused the image of Messiah; images of divine power and presence, God's "word" or "name" or "wisdom;" the image of divine sonship, belonging primarily to the chosen people; the ritual lamb of Atonement; David the viceroy of God; Adam the new-created Image of God. Jesus' teaching revolved especially around two of the greatest Old Testament images:

"kingdom of God," of which something has already been said, and "Son of Man," which is most fully developed in the book of Daniel. Jesus accomplished the decisive transformation of these images himself although it was left to the apostles and evangelists, the Christian prophets, to carry it out.

Farrer points out that what Christ taught and how he taught, the manner and the matter of his teaching, are inseparable. "The parables of the Kingdom," for example, "are not the description of something absent, but a means for apprehending something present in power. They are not verbal substitutes for the substance of the Kingdom, but intellectual instruments by which it may be seized."[33] Christ's parables are images of the present relationship of every person to one or another aspect of the will of God, now active in one who calls himself the Son of Man. A challenge to recognize this presence is the earliest gospel's repeated theme. "He who has ears, let him hear!" Here is a riddle, a parable, a dark saying. It must not only be listened to but understood. To hear, to grasp its meaning, is to grasp the kingdom of God, the presence of his sovereign will. That is revelation. What is unveiled is not information but a reality that must be seized, intuited, felt, appropriated.

St Mark attributes to Jesus himself this reluctance to give information, and his own book gives no theoretical exposition of saving truth. Rather, he shows how Christ's life was a visible parable or enacted image of that truth, the present advent of the divine majesty. The enigmatic quality of the earliest gospel strikes nearly every serious reader. For Farrer this mysteriousness is quite deliberate on St Mark's part: the evangelist invites those who read to share in the inspired rebirth of images. Whatever he does, St Mark is not about to set out his message as a take-it-or-leave-it proposition. For Farrer, his gospel resists the very idea that revelation is what anybody merely says, even if the speaker be Jesus himself.[34]

Nor is revelation simply what anybody does or suffers, not even Jesus. By themselves events are dumb. The execution of a certain rabbi from Nazareth, for example, is not in and of itself the salvation of the world. That event had to be commented upon, interpreted, and related to the whole of the previous history of God's dealings with his people. This process of understanding the factual events as the work of God depends on inspiration; from the human side, it depends on imagination. The facts of Christ's life transformed the meaning of the ancient image of God's kingdom, yet the facts themselves "did not *dictate* the fresh way in which the kingdom of God was seen; it had to be imagined."[35] If the events were true works of God, they are *words* as well. They communicate a meaning if and when they are understood. Through certain happenings in the first century, "God in Christ has written the text of a riddle,"[36] and St Mark has written his book to set out in a poetic way the intelligibility of that riddle.

The New Testament poses many such riddles. "What sort of David can it be," Farrer asks, "who is also the martyred Israel and the Lamb of sacrifice? What sort of new Adam can it be, who is also the temple of God? And what sort of living temple can it be, who is also the Word of God whereby the world was made?"[37] But whereas the Gospels of Matthew and Luke smooth the way by providing answers to St Mark's riddles, the earlier book is what Farrer calls a systematic enigma. Its imaginative patterning of event and image allows, but does not force, an underlying meaning to be discerned. He who has ears will be able to understand.

Does Farrer throw over the whole idea of getting at historical information? By no means. Certain events did occur, and the study of the New Testament as a historical record can try to establish what they are. This is a valuable work in itself, but Farrer thinks that "it is not surprising if it fails to find either the voice of God or the substance of supernatural mystery." As he reports Jesus' intention of the parables, so St Mark intends his own gospel; it is for those who have ears. "We have to listen to the Spirit speaking divine things," Farrer continues, "and the way to appreciate his speech is to quicken our minds with the life of the inspired images."[38]

In sum, St Mark is the most unpretentious of the four evangelists, but through what look like very casual words he conveys deep meaning. His gospel is not just a learned acrostic, Farrer insists, but neither is it at all straightforward. He gives his readers events *and* images, history and teaching. The images interpret the events, the events interpret the images, and the interplay of the two is revelation. Both, according to Farrer, have their source in Jesus Christ, who "both performed the primary action and gave the primary interpretation: the apostles," and after them St Mark, "worked out both the saving action and the revealing interpretation."[39] The enigmatic quality of the earliest gospel is part of the reason for Farrer's avowal that, among the four evangelists, "I dearly and specially love St. Mark."[40] His is the gospel that mirrors Christ through riddles. The next section will explore a specific example, the curious ending of the book, to which Farrer brings his methods of poetical interpretation.

§4

Again and again in his enigmatic poem St Mark puts two things side by side, leaving to the reader the task of divining the meaning of their relationship. Sometimes sayings are juxtaposed in this fashion, sometimes images; always the purpose is "to provide the reader with an opportunity and stimulus to reason from analogy."[41] An extended example of this technique appears at the very end of his book, where St Mark has set in parallel two episodes, the sequences of events immediately before and immediately after the Passion narrative. The comparison, as Farrer lays it out in *The Glass of Vision*, is summarized in the following table.[42]

MARK 14: 1 – 52	MARK 16: 8 – 8
A *woman* anoints Jesus's body with *perfume;*	Joseph of Armathea obtains the *crucified body* of Jesus wrapping it in a *linen cloth.*
Jesus tells her that she has *anointed him for burial.*	
At supper, Jesus breaks bread, telling the disciples, *"This is my body,"* and that he will *go before them into Galilee.*	*Three women* bring *perfumes* with which to *anoint it* for (proper) *burial.*
In the garden Jesus tells the disciples, especially *three* of them, to watch.	They see a *lad clad* in a white stole, who recalls Jesus' promise to *go before them into Galilee.*
But they forsake Jesus and *flee,* including a *lad clad* in a *linen cloth.*	The women *flee,* for they are afraid.

The first and much longer sequence tells how a woman brought a jar of nard and anointed Jesus while he was at supper. This, he said, was a good work, since they would not have him always; indeed, she had anointed his body beforehand for burial. Following this, in the Last Supper narrative, Jesus gives his disciples his sacramental body and promises that after he is risen he will precede them into Galilee. Then he admonishes them, three of them especially, to be on their guard in Gethsemane. But the catastrophe takes them unprepared. Everyone forsakes Jesus and flees, among them a youth who leaves in his pursuers' hands the linen cloth with which he was clothed.

In the second sequence Joseph obtains from Pilate the body of Jesus and, after wrapping it in a linen cloth, he buries it. After the Sabbath three women, bringing perfumes to anoint Jesus' body, see at the tomb a youth clothed in white. He bids them tell the disciples that Jesus goes before them into Galilee, as he had promised at the supper. Saying nothing to anyone, however, the women flee because they are afraid.

Farrer begins by calling attention to a number of features common to the two episodes, particularly the ones italicized above. These are not coincidental, but deliberate poetic echoes. An otherwise minor detail lends weight to this proposal, for each of the episodes includes two words, "linen cloth" and "lad," used nowhere else in the whole book. It is as though St Mark were deliberately calling attention to a parallel he wants his readers to perceive between the sequences in which these two words occur.

These episodes are meant to interact in the reader's mind, and Farrer finds that they resonate in a fourfold "poetic persuasion." *First*, the anointing at Bethany was, by anticipation, Jesus' burial anointing. Yet the women on the Sunday after his death try to do what Jesus said had already been done. *Second,* Jesus had already given his disciples his crucified body, in a heavenly manner, when they broke bread together in the upper room. Yet the disciples later attempt to secure the crucified body in an earthly manner, by sealing it in the tomb. *Third,* Jesus had promised that he would go before them into Galilee. Yet they go looking for him outside the walls of Jerusalem and have to be reminded of his promise. *Fourth,* Jesus had warned many times in advance of his coming suffering and death, and had always promised that he would rise again. Yet when the disaster begins in the garden on the night of Judas's betrayal, the disciples — three of them in particular — flee in fear. Similarly after three days, when the promised joy dawns, the three women flee because they are afraid.

What point is made by this "poetical persuasion"? It is that God's action "always overthrows human expectation: the Cross defeats our hope: the Resurrection terrifies our despair . . . no man knows what to do with the divine when it falls into his hands."[43] Of course the women flee. So do we always react to the eternal newness of divine love.

Farrer's account so far leaves an important question unanswered. Poetic or not, is this a fitting note on which to end a book of the good news in Christ? Can St Mark conceivably have stopped with the women's terrified flight? New Testament scholarship has established that the genuinely Marcan text goes no further, and that the remaining verses are a later addition. Farrer agrees that the last words that have any claim to authenticity are " . . . they said nothing to anyone, for they were afraid" (Mk. 16:8). To many this abrupt finish seems inappropriate and various hypotheses have been invented, some more fanciful than others, to account for what appears to be at best an unsatisfactory ending to the earliest gospel. It has been proposed that the evangelist really wrote another page, but it has been lost somehow. Or perhaps, as Farrer jokingly describes it,

> just as St. Mark reached the words 'for they were afraid,' a heavy official hand descended on his shoulder, and a heavy official voice pronounced the fateful words: 'Here, what's all this? You'd better come along with me to the praetorium,' and so the saint's literary career came to an abrupt conclusion.[44]

These guesses are plausible only because the Gospel of Mark is often read through eyes accustomed to the way the Gospels of Matthew and Luke carry the story of Jesus beyond the empty tomb. Their version has come to be the standard of what "should" be included in a gospel. So St Mark "must" have written more than has survived; at least, he must have intended to write more. Probably the twelve verses that continue the Marcan narrative in some versions are themselves the effort of a later scribe who had his own ideas of what "should" have been written, and who brought Mark into line with the other gospels by supplying resurrection appearances of Jesus.

Farrer, however, prefers working in the light to guessing in the dark. His own judgment is based not on what St Mark "should" have written but on what he did write — in the rest of his book. Neither the endings of Matthew and Luke, nor the more general idea that stories should have happy endings, is relevant. Since St Mark wrote before any of the other evangelists, he had no models to imitate; in the second place, what if he never intended to write a story, in the usual sense, at all? What if he is composing, throughout his book, an imaginative poem in narrative form? In one of his best sermons, Farrer offers this imaginary dialogue with the evangelist he "dearly and specially loved."

What? I say to the venerable Evangelist, so your gospel is complete, after all? Yes, says St Mark: I wrote no more. The women ran from the tomb, and held their tongues . . . There was no need for me to tell the Church that Jesus, risen as he had promised, sent his apostles forth into all the world.

Well, if you take that line, I reply, there was no need for you to tell the Church anything: the Church knows. We thought you had written your book to help the Church know what she knows, placarding Christ before her very eyes, and pouring the word of life into her ears. Where is your gospel of the resurrection?

How shall I make you see the resurrection? he replied. I show you, in all my book, the kingship of God present in the action of a man.[45]

In this quotation, Farrer hints at two proposals worked out in detail in his scholarly studies. They are that St Mark had been writing about the resurrection of Christ from the very beginning of his gospel, and that he knew when to stop. The second of these has an interesting parallel in a comment the philosopher Ludwig Wittgenstein makes about one of his own books: "My work consists of two parts: the one presented here plus all that I have *not* written. *And it is precisely that second part that is the important one.*"[46] Farrer finds something similar in the way St Mark respects the limitation of all human words used in conveying divine truth. The appearances of the risen Christ belong to credal statements, for they are the foundation of faith; they do not belong in a narrative, for they cannot be described.

Christ's rising is unique. It cannot be reduced to any other kind of event, and so it cannot be classified. It is just itself. As the second section above suggested, Farrer thinks the only way to describe something unique is to say what it is *like*. "How shall I make you see the resurrection?" St Mark cannot do it directly; instead, he uses a poetic interplay of images, correcting one with another. He develops his own rhythms which work their way into our imagination and which finally carry us right off the last page and into the really important part of his message, the part St Mark did *not* write down. Every sentence in the gospel, Farrer maintains, "points a finger towards it, but the poem ends with finality at the words 'for they were afraid'. The rest cannot be written."[47]

The resurrection cannot be written in the sense that no single image can symbolize it adequately. Instead, the evangelist sets vibrating all of the lesser images of his poem, by combining, contrasting, and expanding their connotations. The perceptive reader, "he who has ears," can follow these repetitions and developments as all of St Mark's images gather together and converge at one point, the unimaginable reality to which "every sentence in the gospel points a finger," but which is not itself in the text. Page by page, St Mark brings his readers to the brink of mystery, to the very edge of what language — even the language of inspired poetry — can express.

He starts with the first verse of his gospel, which seems to be nothing more than the announcement of a lesson: "Here beginneth the Gospel of Jesus, Messiah and Son of God." We might expect that the next line would continue in proper scriptural fashion, with something like "in the days of Pontius Pilate the governor it came to pass . . ." St Mark does not, however, go on in scriptural fashion. He goes to scripture itself, for the beginning of the Gospel of Jesus lies in the prophetic writings. What appears at first as a kind of introductory title is in fact a poetic statement of his theology. "The beginning of the *blessed message* concerning Jesus Christ, according to the text of Isaiah the prophet: See, I send my *messenger* . . . "[48] The text becomes the advent of John the Baptist, for as the next sentence makes clear, John is the messenger foretold by the prophet.

In his first pair of sentences St Mark has presented prefiguration and fulfillment, anticipation and enactment, a riddle and its answer, the imagery of the former dispensation reborn in proclaiming Christ. This twofold scheme he at once repeats, as the messenger utters his own prophecy. One greater than I is coming, he says, with a baptism better than mine. Here is a new riddle — whom does the Baptist mean? — and again the answer follows immediately. Jesus comes from Nazareth and is anointed with the Spirit as well as with water. At the same time a heavenly voice claims him as a son, and so both of the titles announced in the first verse have been bestowed. Jesus is Messiah, Anointed, and he is Son of God. St Mark then sets out a third pair. Jesus, like his forerunner John, enters the wilderness, the wilderness that recalls to Israel's heirs the place of their ancestors' wandering. In the wilderness God's people tempted him; now God's Son himself is tempted by the devil. Jesus, however, succeeds where Israel failed; he overcomes diabolical temptation and at once begins to preach, as John had done, the kingdom, the inheritance of David's throne, the promised land. Here is a summary of Farrer's account in *A Study in St Mark* of the alternating rhythm set in motion by the first few verses of St Mark's poetry:

The beginning of the joyful *message* of Jesus, the *Anointed*, the *Son of God:*

In the *wilderness*, John the Baptist preaches the *kingdom* and a baptism of *repentance*.

a *messenger* to *prepare* the way, crying in the *wilderness*, *prepare* the way of the Lord.

The Baptist foretells the coming of one mightier than he, whose baptism with the *Spirit* will surpass baptism with *water.*

Jesus comes and is baptized with *water;* at the same time he is *anointed* with the *Spirit.* A heavenly voice declares him *Son of God.*

Like the Baptist, Jesus enters the *wilderness,* where he is *tempted* by Satan.

Like the Baptist, Jesus begins to preach the joyful *message of repentance* and the *kingdom.*

Having familiarized his readers with the kind of poetical persuasion he favors, by repeating it three times over, St Mark proceeds to develop the same rhythm as he elaborates on his themes. Farrer summarizes the movement this way: "As water to spirit, as wilderness to promised land, as the defeat of Satanic temptation is to the proclamation of the gospel, so is the act of exorcism to the act of 'raising up'."[49] Among the first events of Jesus' ministry, St Mark records a healing. More exactly, he relates a pair of healings, following the cleansing of the man possessed by unclean spirits with the "raising up" of Simon's mother-in-law. To emphasize their connectedness, he continues with a similar pair of healings: the cleansing of a man from the unclean disease of leprosy and the raising up of the paralytic.

Farrer attributes to the healing miracles a special significance in St Mark's symbolic pattern. These healings form a cumulative prelude to the last and greatest of the healings, the raising up of Jesus himself. Furthermore there are twelve such episodes in St Mark's gospel; twelve individual Israelites are healed by Jesus. St Mark also tells us there were other healings. Why, Farrer asks, has he chosen to record in detail just these twelve? Are these stories simply unrelated set-pieces, variations of a traditional way to narrate miraculous cures?

The clue is the number itself. "To one who has travelled in that region of Jewish writing which forms the background to the New Testament, it becomes almost a routine principle, if he is losing his way, to stop and count."[50] There are twelve Israelites healed, and twelve is the number that symbolizes Israel itself, the twelvefold people descended from Jacob's twelve sons. The Old Testament maintains this symbolic wholeness even when it is necessary to juggle the names of the tribes in order to keep this number. In the gospels the same symbolism is transferred to the apostles, the twelve heads of a new Israel.

The rhythm of St Mark's book is, in part, the product of the simplest of all poetic devices — repetition. But it is not meaningless repetition. Although he revises its details, Farrer's consistent argument is that the number twelve lends symbolic significance to the healing miracles as a series, and brings them into a parallel with the number of the apostles. "The Evangelist who describes Christ's healing mission to the twelvefold people Israel in twelve particular stories of healing also describes a . . . mission to the same people administered by Christ through the twelve apostles."[51] Part of the apostles' mission involves yet another set of twelve. St Mark tells how they distribute twelve loaves, first seven and then five, to the multitudes. He heightens the symbolism of the two stories of miraculous feeding by emphasizing Jesus' use of actions that could have only one meaning for Christian readers. Jesus takes the twelve loaves of bread, blesses them, breaks them, and distributes them through the twelve apostles he has called.

"Against our expectation, and perhaps somewhat against our wills," Farrer writes in the later of his two studies of St Mark's gospel, "we are driven to recognize that the formal skeleton of St Mark's symbolism is arithmetical."[52] The pattern of the healings is primary. In relation to that pattern, which extends throughout the first half of the gospel, the patterns of loaves and apostles take on specific meaning.

The last individual healing does not occur until the very end of this first half, the part of the gospel that has been called a preface to its Passion story. When Jesus heals blind Bartimaeus just before entering Jerusalem, the series is complete. Immediately St Mark begins his account of the greatest enigma, the most stupendous riddle of all: the king who comes in the name of the Lord will be executed. The final healing marks a shift in St Mark's story. Jesus has called and sent and healed and fed all Israel, God's people, David's kingdom. Now the Son of Man himself must suffer. When he is raised up, as he raised up Simon's mother-in-law and the paralytic, a new Israel will rise with him.

St Mark's book condenses to a point. Everything he describes before the first Easter foreshadows the fruits of the resurrection. The life of the world to come, the fullness of Christ's rising, is calling, healing, feeding; the call to discipleship, the healing of the nations, the feeding with bread from heaven. What is the pivot point itself? It is the resurrection. But what is the resurrection? St Mark does not portray it, but he has given his readers in advance the images through which they can grasp that indescribable point. "What is the resurrection?" means "what is it *like*?"

Through his progressive symbolism St Mark says that it is like the healings, for it is "seeing eyes, open ears and a praising tongue."[53] The healings constitute a cumulative series that anticipates Christ's death and resurrection and they foreshadow its fruits as well. Resurrection is like the raising up of Simon's mother-in-law, and, still more, it is like the raising up of Jairus's daughter from death itself. There are other clues; St Mark suggests that the reality of the resurrection is known in the eucharistic meal. Resurrection is carried forward by the apostolic preaching of the joyful message, and by the bringing of many into the rhythm of repentance and belief. How can all of this be expressed? As Farrer imagines St Mark asking, "How shall I make you see the resurrection?" This is how, the evangelist continues, "I show you, in all my book," as much as language can convey:

> the kingship of God present in the action of a man . . . I can show you — I *have* shown you — God in man defeating death, by dying. It is a story as much human as it is divine. The rest is not a story, and I cannot tell it — not, that is, the story of Jesus, and what it was for him to rise from the dead. Of course I can tell you — others will doubtless tell — the story of his disciples, and what it was for them to be shone upon by the new light of Christ's resurrection; for in that story we all of us still live.[54]

How shall I make you see the resurrection?

As water is to spirit, as wilderness to promised land, as the defeat of Satanic temptation to the proclamation of the gospel, as exorcism to raising up, as buried seed to hundredfold harvest, as blindness to sight, incomprehension to revelation, repentance to belief, so also is the death of Christ to ——.

The rest cannot be written. It can be named, of course. It is called resurrection, the life of the world to come, the kingdom. But those are only another set of images. Farrer's comment in a wholly different context is also appropriate here: "If we wish to think on, we must return humbly to the bottom of the ladder, and climb again."

§5

Austin Farrer's biblical studies are certainly not in the mainstream of New Testament study, which is another way of saying they are highly original. It is not surprising that they have not met with unanimous approval; far from it. The refrain of the critical chorus is that his interpretations are too fanciful, too speculative, too elaborate. Even favorable comments call attention to his "puckishness" and "naughtiness," and not a few critics have concluded that Farrer's own imagination is a great deal more lively and subtle than St Mark's. He sees pictures in the clouds — patterns, that is, where none were intended.

A more serious complaint is that Farrer insists on turning every word of the earliest gospel into an allegory. Not only has he found that St Mark juggles a highly complex set of symbols, Old Testament allusions, cross-references, puns, numerical schemes and riddles; Farrer also proposes that the evangelist juggled all of these in order to convey some purely "mystical" meaning. To be sure, Farrer is deeply concerned with the spiritual meaning of scripture. And if he did think that St Mark's intended meaning were somehow independent of the facts his gospel records, Farrer could justly be accused of allegorizing, of taking the Marcan narrative as nothing more than a literary vehicle for eternal verities that can get along quite well without history.

But he thinks nothing of the sort. If anything, Farrer's judgment on what the gospel facts were is more conservative than that of most other New Testament scholars, and he never questions St Mark's having used his words to get hold of those historical facts. He also maintains, though, that God has used the facts of history to signify further facts, facts about himself, and that we are "to use these historical facts in order to get hold of the supernatural or divine facts which God has expressed through them."[55] Emphasis on the spiritual dimension of the Gospel of Mark is not equivalent to de-emphasis of historical events. It is, rather, to ask what those events *mean*. Who was this Jesus, dead and now alive? What has his coming to do with the human-divine relationship? The earliest evangelist was prompted to answer such questions by interpreting the facts through imagery and by reinterpreting images through events. St Mark relates Christ's healings not as a list but as an unfolding series. Does that mean he did not suppose they occurred? By no means. Jesus *did* heal the sick, but so have many others. The healings are important only if they reveal the identity of the healer not as a wonder-worker, but as Messiah. So St Mark undertakes to show through symbolism that the healings were one aspect of a coherent pattern of divine salvation, the act of God the Creator who "makes something from nothing, who raises the dead."[56]

Farrer's approach to scripture is rooted in the conviction that inspired imagination is part of the process by which God discloses himself. "Belief in inspiration," he writes, "is a metaphysical belief; it is the belief that the Creator everywhere underlies the creature, with the added faith that at certain points he acts in, as, and through the creature's mind."[57] That St Mark's act of imagination was God's act of inspiration is precisely the kind of paradox discussed in the first lecture: the paradox of two agents, divine and human, operating together in one activity.

The validity of Farrer's methods of interpretation depends therefore on a prior question. Is inspiration, understood in this way, a reality? Is there any experimental proof of such a phenomenon? This is just the same question as the one posed in the first lecture about creation, when the answer was that divine creativity can only be ascertained by personal experiment. The more particular case of inspiration is quite similar for, like creation, inspiration is a present experience. None of us is called to write a new gospel, but all of us must take part in the revelation begun in and through Jesus and continued by the evangelists.

Farrer takes very seriously St Paul's statement that "we have the mind of Christ" (I Cor. 2:15). He writes that "the extension of the revelation beyond the person of Christ Himself, involves the extension of the 'mind of Christ' to His disciples; and this extension is not simply their taking His words to heart, it is the operation in them of a divine presence."[58] This is so, moreover, whether the disciples belong to the first century or the twentieth. Even when they qualify it with all due modesty, Christians today must uphold the claim that they too have a divine gift. Indeed, if the gospel is credible to anyone it is *because* of such a gift, because some touch of the supernatural presence that the gospel describes has acted in the mind.

From the believer's point of view, is there any need for Farrer's complex analysis of the Gospel of Mark or for his metaphysical account of inspiration? As to the first point, St Mark's book is by no means so simple as some have thought it to be, and at a distance of nineteen centuries his deliberate riddles have become all the more mysterious. As to the second, Farrer considers that anyone "who has felt, even in the least degree, the power of these texts to enliven the soul and to open the gates of heaven must have some curiosity about the manner in which the miracle is worked."[59]

Farrer does not offer his scholarly books as a substitute for attention to the scriptures themselves. He is well aware that Christians have always turned from the theologians and philosophers who talk about God, to the Bible where they hope to find God's Spirit. Yet the ideas of philosophers and theologians do influence Christians, not least by shaping what they hear from the pulpit. Farrer points out that what we believe, implicitly or explicitly, about the way God acts determines what we believe about his inspiration of scripture and that, in turn, determines the use to which we put the Bible.

How then do Farrer's studies, erudite and theological as they often are, bear upon the spiritual use of scripture? *The Triple Victory* and some of his sermons provide the best answer, since they show the practical side of his scriptural divinity. Here, however, three questions should be asked.

(1) What should be looked for in scripture? We look to the Bible for saving truth, of course, but we will not find it in St Luke's dates or St John's geography. We read the historical information in order to grasp what God has said through what happened. The Bible, according to Farrer, should be read in great sweeps, and it should be read backwards. The Old Testament is revealing because it is the alphabet of images which the New Testament authors use to spell out the meaning of Christ. The multiplicity of figures, prophecies, and hopes all came to a focus in the story of Jesus, in whom all the images are reborn. Especially in the Gospel of Mark, the story of Jesus itself focuses on a single unimaginable point, outside time and without dimension: the exaltation of the Son of Man. Proof-texts will not reveal Christ in the Old Testament, but he can be found there by those whose imaginations are quickened. As Farrer's comparison of scripture with poetry suggests, reading the Bible is an art rather than a science.

(2) How can the spiritual meaning of scripture be discerned? Reading the Bible will, on Farrer's principles, be

first of all meditative, the immersion of oneself in the images on the page just as they stand. Reading in great sweeps is thus complemented by attention to single images. This does not mean that Farrer holds a doctrine of literal inspiration in the sense that every word of the Bible is guaranteed to be free from human error. He does, however, hold that "inspiration is to be found in the very words and . . . not in any general (and therefore dead) ideas."[60] Rational theology can endeavor to understand the metaphysical aspect of revelation, showing how divine initiative and human response, inspiration and imagination, coinhere. But such an account is altogether formal. It does nothing to elucidate the content of revelation: that is to be found in what the New Testament authors wrote.

If Farrer's analyses of St Mark's gospel and St John's Apocalypse are substantially correct, there is every reason to think that attentive and thoughtful reading is just what these authors expected of their readers. None of the New Testament writers thought that their books were "going to be read once to the congregations and then used to wrap up fish, like a pastoral letter."[61] There is no end to what can be learned from seemingly incidental bits of narrative, and the smallest detail may be the clue to important disclosures.

At the same time, St Mark's riddles are not mere puzzles. Like any poet, he is out not only to say something but also to *do* something — to change his readers. The contemplative attitude Farrer advocates is not idle curiosity. What is revealed in the earliest gospel's interplay of event and image is the Will behind the world; through the scriptural glass God claims the wills of those who read. In the same sermon that includes his imaginary dialogue with St Mark, Farrer recommends the simple and traditional form of prayer that consists in taking gospel scenes and "living oneself into them." St Mark's gospel itself is a great enacted parable, and those who live themselves into it participate in its revelation. But they are also called to live the parable. The literary pattern of the earliest gospel mirrors the rhythm of God's saving action, and into that action St Mark draws his readers.

More than imagination, then, is reborn through such reading. The intention and form of our own living become continuations of those realities to which the gospel's images refer. Believing is, for Farrer, always living what we believe, and Christians believe not just in God but in his saving Incarnation. Through revealed images we believe in that divine reality, and in living the parables of it we believe what they reveal. We do not simply read the life of Christ. We enter into it.

> By sympathy and by a well-controlled use of imagination we identify ourselves with Christ's act or attitude in the narrative before us.
> Nor is that all. We do not simply enter into the recorded history of Christ, as we might enter into the destiny of a tragic hero, set before us on the stage. We make his action ours, or rather (as we think it truer to say) he takes our action into his own.[62]

(3) Farrer's mention of well-controlled imagination leads to a final remark. To this point it would seem that reading scripture is a highly individualistic activity liable to exaggeration and personal whim. Farrer's understanding of the continuity of revelation implies, on the contrary, that no one who reads the Bible must or should do so in solitude. While it is true that

> *God is his own interpreter*
> *And he will make it plain,*

this does not mean that each person has a private access to divine enlightenment or should construe any text according to the feelings or inclinations of the moment. "God is his own interpreter," Farrer allows, "but he does not interpret himself only by speaking in the single reader's mind."[63] It is the community of Christian minds, the Church past and present, to which the individual reader will turn, and thereby turn to the mind of Christ.

Anyone who believes, Farrer writes, believes a gospel which has been believed already, prolonging the belief of others. As the first lecture suggested, he sees the life of faith as a continual experiment with divine creativity in which believers appropriate the experience of others and thus extend the experiment by proxy. For Christianity, the first moment of belief is the same as the first moment of inspiration; both were Christ's, for the recognition of revealing action began with him. Moreover, Christ himself "experimented with creation when he threw himself and all the world's hopes into nothingness, by the death of the cross."[64]

True, we know all of this only through the interpretations of the evangelists. But Farrer does not discount their personal contribution. It forms an indispensable part of the growing understanding of what Christ is, an understanding that will be complete only when we see him face to face. God is his own interpreter in Christ, and for Farrer "the work of revelation, like the whole work of Christ, is the work of the mystical Christ, who embraces both Head and members."[65] We have the mind of one member, expressed in his portion of the revealing work — St Mark's gospel. Through the present gift of the same Spirit who inspired this earliest of evangelists, the pattern of our redemption possesses and molds our minds as it possessed and molded his. And then we have the mind of Christ: *to whom therefore, with the Father and the Holy Spirit, indivisible Trinity and social Unity, be ascribed as is most justly due all might, dominion, majesty and power, henceforth and forever.*

III

CHRIST AND CREATION

And he that sat upon the throne said, Behold, I make all things new. I am Alpha and Omega, the beginning and the end. He that overcometh shall inherit all things; and I will be his God, and he shall be my son.
APOCALYPSE, XXI, 5–7

THINKING ABOUT GOD is a very curious way of thinking. It is nothing like inspecting the cat on the mat or balancing a checkbook, for God is neither a physical object to be scrutinized nor an abstraction to be calculated. Yet people do think about God; only afterward does theology take up the work of organizing and vindicating their thoughts. Perhaps the most important question a theologian can ask is, what leads anyone to think about God in the first place?

Austin Farrer's answer is that religious thinking begins indirectly. The idea of God comes to us along with some other thought, so that thinking about the infinite begins involuntarily. All deliberate thinking, including theological reasoning, builds on spontaneous thinking; it develops thoughts that we just think, thoughts that occur before we ask how or why. Thinking about God is thinking about divine activity displayed in and through something we experience, and the preceding lectures have discussed two ways in which an idea of God imposes itself upon human minds: through creation in the first lecture, through scripture in the second.

In both cases Farrer shows how religious thinking can be focused by a series of refinements like steps of a ladder. Persuade a person to see "the mysterious depth and seriousness of the act by which he and his neighbour exist, and he will have his eyes turned upon the bush in which the supernatural fire appears, and presently he will be prostrating himself with Moses, before him who thus names himself: 'I am that I am'."[1] The thought of God, in other words, naturally accompanies thinking about any finite being; above all it accompanies the thinking involved in moral judgment. This argument is developed in Farrer's rational theology, yet it can also be compared to Bonaventure's description of the ascent of the heart and mind to God.

The second lecture suggested a similar ascent. The Christian gospels tell the story of a man, Jesus of Nazareth. They are powerful simply as stories; in some way they stir our thoughts and feelings, and call for our response. In some way — but how? We can begin with the whole story, as we can begin with the whole creation. But St Mark's version of the good news is not shapeless, though it does not have the kind of plot and structure we might expect. Its movement is symbolic, and it follows Christ's journey towards Jerusalem. The Passion is not just the last item in chronological order, but the goal of the whole book. From a serious wonder about the humanity of Jesus, the earliest evangelist draws his readers to adore Christ's deity in the stupendous riddle of the cross. The Gospel of Mark points beyond itself: the steps leading to the crucifixion lead to God.

The story of the human Jesus, like the riddle of natural creation, is incomplete. We read them aright only if they force upon us the thought of God. Both of them advance to a focus, a point without dimension that can only be understood as the act of God. The summit of the ladder of creation is the mystery of freewill, the paradox of willing the will of God, and the climax of the Christian story is the mystery of the cross, the paradox of death self-destroyed.

Do we need both of these? Granted that their form is similar, is not their content quite disparate? Are these paths to different Gods? For Farrer they are distinct but inseparable, and the purpose of this lecture is to show how Christ and creation converge. His work as a whole makes it very clear that Farrer is not just a philosopher who dabbles in biblical study, nor just an exegetical scholar who dabbles in metaphysics. He makes no such separation and none, he maintains, can be made. His work in scripture and metaphysics reflects a conviction that Christianity worthy of the name has two components. Its center is in Christ and its foundation is creation.

The unity of Christ and creation can be reached by starting either from Farrer's philosophical theology or from his scriptural divinity. The next section will take the second route by suggesting how the rebirth of Old Testament images in the New Testament weaves together God's creative and redemptive activity.

§2

"Creation" and related words are almost absent from the New Testament, and so on the surface it would seem that the Christian message is not deeply concerned with God the Creator. But as the second lecture has suggested,

Farrer argues that biblical thought is not so much conceptual as imaginative, so the occurrence of *words* for creation is neither here nor there. His approach is to ask
whether creation finds expression in New Testament *images*, and he argues that it does. Indeed, the theme of creation is reflected in one of the two images around which
Jesus' own teaching revolves — the title "Son of Man."

There is nothing in biblical studies on which everyone
agrees, and debate about "Son of Man" continues to divide
New Testament scholars. Farrer himself takes the position
that Jesus did apply to himself the title "Son of Man," an
image that had already developed through a long history
and had accumulated rich associations. When Jesus made
it a part of his message, "Son of Man" did not stand for a
simple idea. It had gathered in itself a web of subordinate
images and symbolic resonances. So seriously did he take
this image, according to the Gospel of Mark, that Jesus
chose to die for it. In the high priest's court he did not
simply answer the questions put to him but added a reference to the title he had made his own and thereby, as Farrer puts it, marked out for himself the ground on which he
would erect his cross. The high priest's question was, "Are
you the Christ, the Son of the Blessed?" To this Jesus
answered, "I am; and you will see the Son of man sitting at
the right hand of Power and coming with the clouds of
heaven" (Mk. 14:61–62). This blasphemy was swiftly con-
demned, and the civil governor was persuaded to carry out
the sentence of death.

This, together with other Marcan texts, Farrer takes to
indicate the central importance of "Son of Man" for Jesus'
understanding of himself and his work. What, then, might
this crucial image have meant to him? The words themselves are no help, because no image means anything detached from a context. Rather, the associations of "Son of

Man" made it the appropriate title for Jesus to assume. The speech in the high priest's court refers unambiguously to the most important source of these very intricate associations, the seventh chapter of Daniel:

> I saw in the night visions,
> and behold, with the clouds of heaven
>   there came one like a son of man,
> and he came to the Ancient of Days
>   and was presented before him.
> And to him was given
>   dominion and glory and kingdom,
>   that all peoples, nations, and languages
>   should serve him;
> his dominion is an everlasting dominion,
>   which shall not pass away,
> and his kingdom one
>   that shall not be destroyed.   (Dan. 7:13–14)

To whom does God, the Ancient of Days, give a universal and everlasting kingdom? The answer depends upon the imaginative scheme of the whole book of Daniel, which itself has roots further back in the Old Testament tradition. Farrer's detailed and controversial analysis finds the background and context of Daniel's vision in general, and of the "Son of Man" image in particular, in the creation story of the book of Genesis. The story that provides, directly or indirectly, an imaginative basis for Daniel's "Son of Man" is the story of Adam.[2] As Farrer traces it, the line that runs from Genesis 1 to Daniel 7 follows the subtle laws of poetic association, and only the broadest outlines of his argument can be suggested here.

After the fall of the Israelite and Judaean monarchies, the people struggled to conceive how their humiliation could be understood as the will of their God. Why had the

Lord who brought their ancestors out of bondage allowed a new captivity to befall them? Convinced that the decline of Israel's fortunes was not permanent, the prophets foretold a divine reversal: God would do a "new thing," and restore what had been lost. Later Old Testament books use a variety of images to express this hoped-for renewal. One kind of imagery dwells on the theme of kingship, and tells how God's "new thing" will be the re-establishment of a monarchy ruled by a new and better David. Another depicts the renewal in images from an earlier stage of Israel's history, so that deliverance from Babylon is seen as a new Exodus. In the most sweeping imagery of Israel's hopes, the new thing the Lord will bring to pass is symbolized as nothing less than a new *creation*, a renewal of earthly affairs from the very start. In Isaiah 65, for instance, God announces through the prophet that former things will be forgotten, when the descendants of Jacob will again inherit Jerusalem and serve the Lord there. "For behold, I create new heavens and a new earth . . . be glad and rejoice forever in that which I create; for behold I create Jerusalem a rejoicing, and her people a joy" (Is. 65:17–18).

The book of Daniel is even later than the end of Isaiah. In the situation that Daniel portrays, the priesthood as well as the monarchy have failed. The last link with Israel's former political order is broken, and the tyranny of foreign kings prevails.[3] Yet the hope remains that God will still vindicate his people. In Daniel the "saints of the most high" will triumph at last, and their victory will rest on a foundation deeper than either the Davidic kingship or the Aaronic priesthood. What remains of God's loving rule? In the book of Daniel, the sovereignty of the renewed Israel is the sovereignty of Adam. Its author develops his expectation through images that show the coming victory as a repetition of Genesis itself. In the beginning Adam had been given dominion over the beasts; so would the Son of Man be given dominion and glory and kingdom. At his enthronement the heathen empires, which Daniel symbolizes as composite beasts — a four-headed leopard, a winged lion — will be conquered.

Daniel's vision blends the week of creation from Genesis with its author's own political situation. Daniel does not simply state that the sixth day of creation will happen again; through complex details, its episodes amount to a poetic persuasion that it must happen again. God is faithful and as he acted in the beginning, so will he act once more. This is the center of Farrer's interpretation; the meaning of Daniel's strange poem is to be found in the way it echoes the imagery of Genesis. God, says the prophet, will re-create, and a new Adam will rule in a paradise that shall not fail. What bearing does all of this have on the interpretation of the New Testament? Farrer concludes that "Son of Man," as first-century Jews understood it through the book of Daniel, means the bearer of Adamic rule yet to come.[4]

Daniel's prophecy provides much of the material in Christianity's rebirth of images. It is a source to which St John turns repeatedly for the images out of which he draws his own vision of the future, since God's new creation is also a central theme of the Revelation of John. But before this Christian prophecy of divine consummation was written, Jesus himself had alluded, through Daniel's image "Son of Man," to his people's legend of the creation. His choice of this title amounts to a claim to authority prior to that of the covenant God made with David, prior to his covenant with Moses, and prior even to the covenant with Abraham. By what authority did Jesus teach and act? By authority deriving from the covenant between Adam and God, when at creation the Creator put all things under his feet.

"The significance of Genesis," as Farrer understands it here, is "that it contains this picture of an idea which Christ proved by living it out."[5] As the second lecture has discussed, this picture — the tale of Adam — is a natural theology in images. The author of Genesis expresses in vivid figures the whole fact of created and fallen human existence. Since he is not a metaphysician, he has portrayed as past event what is inescapably real always and everywhere: human beings occupy a certain place in the order of things, we are conscious of failure to fulfill that place, guilt and frustration and inability to reconcile ourselves to the prospect of physical death are our lot. Fountain and wilderness, humanity and the animals, the pain of childbirth and the toil for food, "the image of God to which we are born and the dust into which we resolve" — these are Genesis's images of human finitude. Adam, humankind, is given a destiny. He must order and govern the rest of creation according to the Creator's will, and in this he fails. Is divine purpose ultimately thwarted? The prophecy of Daniel in particular says that it is not, by throwing the whole creation narrative into the future when a new Adam will succeed where Adam's children have failed.

According to Farrer, we must suppose that Jesus of Nazareth also meditated on his own destiny in the light of the Law and the Prophets. Many titles were available in the Jewish traditions, but he chose Daniel's emblem of the Son of Man coming with the clouds of heaven. And Jesus set out to *be* the story that image embodies, the story of Genesis reflected through Daniel. St Mark's gospel shows his acting out of the part of the promised Adam, the Son of Man in Daniel's new creation.[6] In the name of the Son of

Man, created on the sixth day to have dominion over the Sabbath of eternity, Jesus claims jurisdiction over the Sabbath that Israel kept on the seventh day. Because he fulfills Adam, Jesus appeals to the Creator's first intention; against the law that Moses gave for the hardness of the people's heart, he counters that "in the beginning it was not so." He surpasses Adam by refusing the same temptation Adam's enemy had proferred in the garden:

> Do this and that, the serpent had said to Adam, and make yourself your own God. If thou art the Son of God, says the tempter to Christ, do this and that: show your divinity and claim it by self-chosen arbitrary acts of power; subject yourself to me and possess yourself of the universal dominion promised to the Son of Man. No. Adam grabbed, but Christ renounced. The birds have nests and the foxes holes: the Son of Man hath not where to lay his head.[7]

Thus the imaginative ikon of Christ in St Mark's gospel centers on that point at which God creates and humanity is created. Divine creativity is shown in the making of what is most truly human, in the completion of Adam's destiny, in the Son of Man. Adam was made in the image of God; Jesus restored the human image that had been lost.[8] Here is the first link between Christ and creation, and between rational and revealed theology as Farrer perceives them. In what does being made in the image of God consist? Farrer's rational theology argues that we are created creators: our self-making is a faint but real analogy of the self-determining power by which God makes the world.[9] But if it be true that we catch a glimpse of divinity in the highest, most godlike of our own actions, how much more must we say that "if the action of God is anywhere to be seen, it is in the free, the human life of Jesus Christ. The more human it is, the more it is divine; the freer it is, the more it is the will of God."[10] The whole dispensation of God, Farrer observes at the end of his *Study in St Mark*, flows from his creation of humanity, and in one of his sermons he adds that no one knew how human it is possible to be until Adam was remade in Christ.[11]

Farrer thought it a wise saying that there is not a line of theology in the Bible, and this is quite true if by theology is meant only precise and conceptual discourse. None the less the imagery of the New Testament, and of the earliest gospel in particular, has a theological meaning beyond the poetic. His lifelong study of the Gospel of Mark led Farrer to two conclusions about St Mark as a theologian, both of which are somewhat surprising when compared to the general trend of biblical studies. Anticipating the development of redaction criticism, the study of New Testament authors' own theological standpoints, Farrer argues that the earliest evangelist held a consistent christological position. The complex symbolism behind his use of "Son of Man" is the clue to St Mark's own conviction of Jesus' messianic — that is, christological — destiny.

Farrer's second unorthodox conclusion makes the first more specific. "It is common form," he objects, "to discount the testimony of St Paul to the central importance of Adamic Christology. 'This', it is said, 'is St Paul's idiosyncracy. The primitive preaching of Christ knew nothing of it.' "[12] On the contrary, Farrer holds that there is substantial agreement between St Paul and St Mark, the two earliest Christian witnesses, on this most fundamental point of teaching. The message of Christ, both what was preached about Christ and what Christ preached, identifies Jesus of Nazareth with the bearer of Adamic rule.

> Let it be granted that Christ thought in the terms which his inheritance supplied. His inheritance supplied the scripture, and the scripture contained Adam; and Daniel . . . had cast upon the figure of Adam a Messianic light. How could Christ fail to see his destiny in Adamic terms? How else can he have understood himself to be the Saviour of Mankind?[13]

This is Farrer at his most conservative. He does not bring to his biblical studies an assumption that nothing supernatural could have happened, supposing this assumption to be objective and scientific. But the evidence, he believes, will not support the idea of St Mark's as the "simple" gospel, or of Jesus as an ethical teacher and nothing more. To see Christ as the perfection of humanity is one side of the picture. The other, in symbolic language, sees him not only as Son of Man but Son of God. Though Farrer takes this as the basic Christian affirmation, it does not keep him from asking how Christians are to understand what they affirm. It is much less certain that Jesus used "Son of God" of himself than that he used "Son of Man;" what was it that drew from the early church this avowal? Why, for example, does St Mark use it at the beginning of his book and again at the end, in the centurion's acclamation?

§3

In one sense Adam was the child of God, since he had no human ancestors. This idea appears in the genealogy of the Gospel of Luke, which traces Jesus' forebears back through the generations to "Enos, the son of Seth, the son of Adam-the-son-of-God" (Lk. 3:37). Those who heard Jesus preach, moreover, would not have thought it improper to refer to any Israelite as a son of God. But Farrer suggests that Christ's followers came to ask, "This Jesus, what sort of a son is he to God? And they answered, He is a proper Son and so he is what his Father is. His Father is God, and he can be no less."[14]

What had the disciples experienced? Farrer sums up St Mark's account by suggesting that in Jesus they found "the kingship of God present in the action of a man," the complete instance of someone who wills the will of God, a pattern of personal activity "so rooted and grounded in God's will and action as to be the personal life of God Himself, under the self-imposed conditions of a particular human destiny."[15]

Farrer does not suppose that Christ's disciples were rational theologians, but they knew that God was God. And so for them the earthly life of Christ was not something altogether new. Rather, it concentrated a pattern that could be seen darkly elsewhere. This life "did not strike his disciples as an erratic block in the structure of God's purposes . . . What they said amounted to something more like this: 'Here is a group of facts in which whatever else we know of God's designs is focussed and brought to complete expression.' "[16]

Looking back, the first generation of Christians could recognize that Jesus had said as much in his teaching, and in retrospect they realized that he who called himself Son of Man had all along been living the life of a proper child of God. His death and resurrection, most of all, drove them to reflect on Jesus' identity, on who he was, and they were inspired to declare that the Christ is divine. St Mark has set this down poetically by showing how Jesus' dying into life is the unimaginable point where his humanity is completely identified with God the Creator. It is *the* act of God. Yet that rising, St Mark also says, began much earlier. The earliest gospel shows the earthly life of Jesus as an anticipation of his risen life, and the author of the latest gospel puts the same idea in its most striking form. Immediately before his Passion, according to St John's account, Jesus says to Martha, "I *am* the resurrection" (Jn. 12:25). "Does this mean 'I give resurrection,' " Farrer asks, "or 'I rise from the dead'? It means both, and it means more. It means 'I achieve resurrection in myself . . . because of what I am. This is what divine sonship, taking hold of mortal flesh, does to it.' "[17] Here Farrer himself is continuing the process of comparing images. The symbolic equation he draws is this: sonship to God = the new creation of humanity = resurrection.

So human freedom is our general clue to the creation, but Christ is the specific clue. By extension, this is how the groundedness of all finite activity in the divine Will is and should be. Christ crystallizes in his own life the pattern of destiny toward which we feel drawn and toward which God draws all things. For that reason Christ does not only reveal something about ourselves, about the essence of humanity, but also reveals something about God that could not be guessed by rational theology. The superiority of revelation over "natural" religion is, Farrer writes, "precisely this: it tells of the special means God has taken to show us, outside the common course of nature, some part of that great overplus, which exceeds the capacity of nature's looking-glass to reflect it."[18] The clue to creation cannot but be the clue to the Creator.

As Christians were led into fuller understanding of what the experience of Christ had meant, this conviction took shape in the prologue to the fourth and latest gospel, which proclaims that the image enacted by Jesus Christ is the divine pattern, God's self-expression, a word that was in the beginning with God and through which all things are made. In Christ it is revealed that the "heart of God's action is the ceaseless begetting of a life equal to his own; a life, a person worthy of his love, and able to return it."[19] The "great overplus" Farrer speaks of as revealed in Christ is the plurality of the One God: Christ made known the Trinity.

Here again Farrer argues that the New Testament presents divine threeness not through concepts, but through an image. Neither statistics nor word-study are of much help in determining whether or not the Trinity is "in" the New Testament; what we find instead is an image reborn, the image "Son of God." As with "Son of Man," the development of this image is complex, and poetic rather than logical. One aspect of it unfolds beginning with Isaiah's prophecy of a ruler from David's house, a king anointed not with oil but with the Spirit of the Lord. Certain late Jewish writings, with which the New Testament authors appear to have been familiar, elaborate this figure and add to Isaiah's imagery symbols drawn from the story of Abraham. Repeatedly Isaac is designated by Abraham as his only and beloved son. The anointing of a supreme leader to which the *Testaments of the XII Patriarchs* looks forward is an opening of the heavens and a blessing by God "as from Abraham to Isaac."

This composite image is one of the roots from which the Christian doctrine of the Trinity springs. Farrer writes that in the Gospel of Mark we are shown "the whole image become fact in the baptism of Christ. The heavens are now opened indeed, the voice of the Father audibly designates a divine Isaac as his beloved Son, and the spirit of hallowing descends visibly as a dove."[20] The image of anointing and the image of Isaac both contribute to St Mark's "Son of God" symbolism.

There is, however, another strand. The Old Testament applies the image of sonship to God principally to God's people, to Israel itself. By extension the royal psalms refer to Israel's king as God's adopted son. Israel's king *is* Israel, and Israel is God's son; Israel is also Jacob, whose name is the name of his descendants just as the names of his twelve sons are the names of the clans of the children of Israel. In the Gospel of Mark this second strand of "Son of God" imagery informs the passages in which Jesus is himself a new Israel, "our greater Jacob," as Farrer says in one of his poems. The apostles are his "children," through whom he founds a new people of God.

St Mark writes in the first sentence of his book that he is telling the good news of Jesus the Anointed. What follows is a dramatic parable in which the Christ himself enacts Adam, the new-made image of God; Isaac, only and beloved son; David, the anointed viceroy of the Lord; Israel, from whom is born God's people. Because all of this is shown in the pages of the earliest gospel, Farrer argues that there is no need to look to other religious traditions to find why Jesus was believed to be a divine son. We need only look to the tradition Jesus himself knew: the Law, the Prophets, the psalms. His position raises the same question posed at the end of the last section, namely, was it Jesus who thought this way about himself, or was his sonship to God just a product of the early church's devotion?

These are not strict alternatives; it is not for Farrer a question of one or the other. So long as it can be seen as *interpretation* — a development, that is, rather than an addition — of Jesus' words and deeds, the reflection of early Christians is itself an aspect of the process of revelation. Farrer makes this point strikingly in *The Glass of Vision:*

> I will freely confess, for my own part, that unless I thought myself honestly led to recognize in Christ's historical teaching seeds of the doctrine of his divine person and work, then I should not believe. I cannot take these things simply from St. Peter and St. Paul, as their inspired reaction to 'the fact of Christ.'
>
> The choice, use and combination of images made by Christ and the Spirit must be simply a supernatural work: otherwise Christianity is an illusion.[21]

Christian teaching about the Trinity develops the gospels' "Son of God" theme, and that is revealed by Christ through his choice, use and combination of images.

Theological interpretation tries to state what the images grasp, but it cannot replace them with precise words. Theology as Farrer understands it is a set of rules by which the scriptures are to be read, a kind of grammar that relates the elements of its imaginative language. As with any language, knowing the grammar is necessary but it is no substitute for reading. The doctrine of the Trinity is itself such a rule; by itself it cannot be conceptualized. Reflection on scripture concludes that Christians must say what cannot be imagined: that the One who makes himself known in revelation is not solitary, and that God is social yet not divided.

God surpasses himself. This divine "overplus" embodied in Jesus of Nazareth is, in the technical sense of the term, a mystery. We can see *that* it must be true and at the same time we cannot think *how*. "But then, it is not required of us to think the Trinity. We can do better; we can live the Trinity."[22] This remark from one of Farrer's sermons brings back the theme of theology and spirituality. God's self-surpassing is the center of Christian doctrine and for Farrer it is also the heart of Christian living.

§4

The fusion of theological and spiritual concerns in Farrer's own thought is nowhere plainer than in the first sentences of his devotional book *Lord, I Believe.* "Prayer and dogma are inseparable. They alone can explain each other. Either without the other is meaningless and dead." Somewhat later he amplifies this by proposing that "no dogma deserves its place unless it is prayable, and no Christian deserves his dogmas who does not pray them."[23] Devotion and the doctrines of the Christian tradition complement each other everywhere, but especially for Farrer in the case of the Trinity. His is an Augustinian view, in which the only proper human analogy for God is not a society of three persons but a society of two. God is begetter and begotten and a mutuality of interaction so completely given and received that it constitutes that third whom we call Holy Spirit. The basis of this analogy is the Son of God imagery discussed in the last section; that it is the right analogy Farrer finds confirmed in Christian experience.

The Christian religion, according to Farrer, is more than a living relationship to God. If it were only that, what need is there for Christ? Christian spirituality is not adherence to God alone, but to that saving mystery, the great "overplus," which is inseparable from the doctrines of Trinity and Incarnation. Christians confess a savior who is truly divine and truly human, Son of God and Son of Man. In line with this belief, Farrer maintains that if Christians can be said to know anything *qua* Christians, it is their adoption into divine sonship. As the second lecture has emphasized, revelation cannot be simply information and it cannot have taken place only in the past. "The Trinity is revealed to Christians because they are taken into the Trinity." Even more emphatically, Farrer writes that to be in the Trinity *is* Christian existence.[24]

Around this doctrine and this experience all the others gather. Toward this God has providentially led Israel, for Farrer regards the prophetic preparation for Messiah as the "forepart" of Messiah's Incarnation.[25] The Old Testament images of kingship and kingdom are part of this preparation. In Christ, however, these images have been reborn. The Incarnation continues. If in a parable God makes men and women partakers of his kingdom, Farrer writes that "he will, in a more literal form of statement, make them

103

associate with his Godhead."[26] This is the Christian faith: our adoption as children of God depends upon the Sonship that *is* God, Sonship by nature. Association with the Godhead is identity with Jesus Christ and so to live the image and likeness of God is, as Farrer puts it, to live the Trinity.

What can that possibly mean? Once more the question of experiential evidence arises, the problem of giving present meaning to traditional words. The first lecture suggested that our experience of willing the will of God is a kind of ecstasy, or being "outside ourselves," and that prayer is its prime example. Adherents of many religions speak this way of mystical or quasi-mystical experience, but Farrer believes that Christians can say more. For it was by being "outside himself,"

> by being ecstatic in the literal sense of that word that Jesus brought the life of the Blessed Trinity into our world; for it is in ecstasy and in mutual indwelling that the marvellous life of the Godhead consists. God Our Father goes out of himself to be all in his Son — this is the first ecstasy: and the Son goes out of himself to live by that very indwelling of the Father in him — that is the second ecstasy. There is a third ecstasy when there is a creation, and God comes out of himself to be all and everywhere and all things in his creatures. It is the fourth ecstasy, when the creatures of God go out of themselves to be in the God who indwells them. But this ecstasy the creatures of God scarcely achieve, until the Son of God takes on the form of a creature, and lives therein the ecstatic life: and when he died on the cross, he gave it to us for a legacy.[27]

Here Farrer has conjoined Christ and creation, theology and spirituality, and tied all of these to the lived belief of Christians. Our clue to God lies in experience of self-surpassing in which we freely create ourselves, truly express our real being in our actions, and know at the same time that what we have done is the work of a Will supremely worthy of our worship. In such action, Farrer writes, there is no division between the divine and human aspects of creativeness, "for then God's will for his creature and what the creature does are simply the same; the creature is most himself by expressing God."[28]

This, however, we scarcely achieve. Because there are such "ecstatic" moments we know too that our aspirations can be out of tune with the Will behind the world, and this disharmony is sin. It divides what ought to be one and makes us false to ourselves, to the true selves God wills to make us. Like Augustine, Farrer considers that *evil* is the spoiling of some created thing, while *sin* is spoiling the process of creation itself. We come to grips with the real problem, therefore, in the same place we meet the creativity that sin negates — in ourselves. We meet what we cannot explain, resistance to irresistible love. Sin is inexplicable because it is perverse. How, Farrer asks, can sheer unreason be rationalized? "It is the one irreducible surd in the arithmetic of existence."[29] Sin cannot be explained because it has no cause; it is irrational because it is the opposite of what has no opposite, the will of God. Farrer sums up the predicament, interestingly enough, in a sermon about the message of the earliest evangelist:

> Shall we reduce St. Mark's Gospel to three lines?
> God gives you everything.
> Give everything to God.
> You can't.[30]

This is the point beyond which we cannot pass alone, the point where natural theology falters. What does revelation add; what is its answer to the "irreducible surd in the arithmetic of existence?" God's great "overplus" is the gift of the kingdom through the death of the Son of Man. It is typical of Farrer that the passage on ecstasy quoted above ends with a reference to the cross. The Son whose ecstatic life we can live is the Crucified, whom theology calls the second person of the blessed Trinity, and whom the imagery of the New Testament calls the lamb slain from the foundation of the world.

Jesus did not simply adopt the title "Son of Man." He changed it. The Son of Man, he tells the disciples, must suffer. The book of Daniel portrays the Son of Man's triumph; Jesus in the Gospel of Mark knows the cost. Almost half of the earliest gospel is taken up with an account of the Passion. The images that compose St Mark's narrative may point beyond the pages of his book, but they do not bypass the crucifixion. The cross is central to the Christian understanding of what God is and does. Christianity is not only theism, though it is that too. Farrer preaches that Christianity

> is summed up in two pictures: God the creator breathing into man's nostrils the breath of life, God the redeemer dying for man on the cross, and breathing out his life into the keeping of his Father. Creation and crucifixion are the two poles of our faith, and each of them is God.[31]

Far from understanding spirituality as a kind of smorgasbord where all the dishes have different names but taste more or less the same, Farrer thinks that there is something distinctive about Christian spirituality. It is on this point, the cross, that Christianity parts company from other religious traditions. One of the greatest modern exponents of Zen Buddhism, D.T. Suzuki, has pointed quite clearly to the difference. A number of his essays relate the experiences of Zen practice to those of Christian mystics, and Suzuki finds much that is common to Christian and Buddhist spirituality. In one of these essays, however, he acknowledges how deeply the second of Farrer's two pictures perplexes and repels him. "Whenever I see a crucified figure of Christ," Suzuki writes, "I cannot help thinking of the gap that lies deep between Christianity and Buddhism . . . To the oriental mind, the sight is almost unbearable."[32]

The cross, and the reality for which it stands, cannot be embraced by Buddhist spirituality. If this is what Christians mean by God, then in spite of similarities between Zen meditation and Christian prayer, there is a very fundamental difference. "The Son of Man must suffer."

"We identify ourselves with what we adore." Here Farrer echoes Augustine's observation that the gist of religion is the imitation of the one who is worshiped.[33] Christianity worships the Creator and the Crucified. Can this object of worship be imitated? Imitation has come to mean feigning or shamming, so Farrer prefers to say that "Christ's dying into life has the power to carry us all through the same motions, and so what we have to do is not simply to imitate but to adhere."[34]

Adherence is a key word in Farrer's vocabulary. To adhere means to participate rather than to copy. It means to identify with and enter into the will of God that is God himself. The first lecture has already discussed the adherence that takes place at the "apex of the will," and now it must be added that Christian spirituality is not just adherence to God but to the Trinity, to the will of God in Christ. A closely-related phrase that turns up frequently in Farrer's work is "the crucifixion of the will." It is a disturbing expression, yet no one who has tried sincerely to seek the divine will in prayer will deny that his or her own willfulness is the first thing that interferes. Effectual prayer takes place when it is not we ourselves who form our prayers, but Another who prays in us. Christians know that Other, the maker of heaven and earth, in one who was crucified for them under Pontius Pilate.

So Farrer's theism hinges on freewill, his Christian theism on that will crucified. "The evidence of faith (I talk of what I think I know) is the evidence of Almighty Power, to break and to heal the will."[35] Nor is this experience

107

peculiar to Farrer. Does not St Paul describe his own adherence to God's saving act in similar terms? "With
Christ," he writes, "I am co-crucified. I live no more;
Christ lives in me" (Gal. 2:20). Salvation, Farrer continues,
cannot be achieved without the use of force. We expose
ourselves to the force of God, but this includes applying
force to ourselves. Adhering to his saving action is costly.
It costs, Farrer suggests,

> the abandonment of a false attitude, it costs a struggle against
> despair of virtue, a sacrifice of the pride which attaches us to
> the defense of our conduct, all the amends we can make to per-
> sons we have wronged — what else? The catalogue could be
> greatly lengthened. Such are the costs of our reconciliation,
> and such costs as these are not remitted to us, even by the
> sacrifice of Christ. We have all these things to do, only that
> Christ's initiative sets us in motion. He took us, and associated
> us with his divine life, even while we struggled against him.[36]

It is by association, imitation, identification, adherence
that we claim our adoption into the Triune God.

A good deal has been said in these lectures about the
importance Farrer gives to images in our knowledge of
God, and about the revolution in imagination that must
occur before anyone can appreciate the New Testament's
revealed truth. Both of these set Farrer somewhat apart
from the theologians who in recent years have called for
Christian language to be demythologized and replaced by
up-to-date, non-mythical terms. In Farrer's estimation this
is a hopeless project, since there is no way to get behind the
revealing images by substituting another set of words. Imagery can be refined and explained, to be sure, and much
of the present lecture has been devoted to showing how
Farrer uses the conclusions of his rational theology to
clarify and understand the meaning of some difficult New
Testament themes. If "myth" means the use of finite symbols for God, there can be no elimination of mythology.
What other symbols are there?

Yet Farrer is willing to speak of demythologization and he regards it as essential — not in theology, however, but in prayer. We must begin with full and vigorous images, with imaginative reliving of the gospels' ikon of Christ, because when we begin to pray we have not yet experienced the reality those images reveal. But even the imagination must be crucified, in prayer and in the life that is animated by prayer.

> The promise of God's dealing with us through grace can be set before us in nothing but images . . . When we proceed to live the promises out, the images are crucified by the reality, slowly and progressively, never completely, and not always without pain: yet the reality is better than the images. Jesus Christ clothed himself in all the images of messianic promise, and in living them out, crucified them: but the crucifed reality is better than the figures of prophecy.[37]

This section has suggested how Farrer connects experiential "proof" of the Trinitarian mystery with both crucifixion and resurrection. They are ultimately two aspects of one reality, or rather two approaches to what transcends human words. Here and now, Farrer writes, "the crucifixion of the will is immortality and glory, and the enjoyment of our heavenly adoption."[38] Neither the Trinity nor human participation in that community of love can properly be described. The Trinity revealed is the Trinity in whom we live, and by whom we are constantly being created and re-created. In one sense the creation of humanity is finished, for the image of God is perfected in what Christ does and suffers. In another sense, Farrer holds, there is no end to divine creativity, no end to our growing up into the image of Christ. Now we see through a glass in a riddle; but then, face to face.

§5

Austin Farrer's work is impossible to pigeonhole. It is at once disturbingly traditional and highly original. After his *Study in St Mark* was published, reviewers suggested that there was nothing in the book that Origen had not thought of seventeen hundred years before. Today the parallel tables and thematic correspondences that fill the pages of Farrer's biblical studies are the stock in trade of structuralism, the most recent development in the interpretation of narratives. Similarly with his philosophical theology: *Finite and Infinite*, thought to be Thomism pure and simple when it was published, can with the clarity of hindsight be seen to address theological questions raised by contemporary "linguistic action" philosophies.

Farrer was an original thinker who avoided novelty. What, after all, can a theologian discover? Presumably God is ever the same, and while human understanding of his ways may hope to become clearer, Farrer nevertheless thinks that revolutions in Christian theism are not to be expected. Natural science achieves "breakthroughs" — theology does not. This is not to say that he contents himself with parroting what has been said before. Christian belief must be lived and thought and prayed differently in different times and places; very seldom does Farrer succumb to the characteristically Anglican disease of antiquarianism.

In his memorial address, Basil Mitchell says that Farrer was an embarrassment "to anyone making *any* sort of list; one simply had to name the others and then add, 'And then, of course, there's Austin Farrer.' "[39] Only a handful of footnotes can be found in all his publications, and the explanation for this disregard of academic convention is that he wanted his arguments to stand on their own persuasiveness rather than on scholarly authority. Farrer draws on many predecessors, ancient and modern, but he writes only what convinces him.

And he writes in order to convince. There is an element of rhetoric even in his most dispassionate books. It is most evident in *The Glass of Vision*, but this began as a set of lectures and lectures, Farrer remarks, are in fact rhetorical. His lapsing into "sermon talk" and his casting of arguments into the form of dialogues have annoyed some critics, and it is true that these devices make it difficult at times to extract a neatly organized series of precise statements. The dialogues, however, serve a purpose; by developing his own points in conversation with alternatives and objections, Farrer exposes the strengths and weaknesses of both sides. Candor and reasonableness are his criteria.

As to Farrer's "sermon talk," amounting at times to piousness, that too has a reason. He has no sympathy for a pseudo-theology that, "neglecting the true Jacob's-ladder of living religion" because it seems creaky and unsafe, builds instead "Babel-towers of spurious demonstration." But though rational argument alone seldom produces conviction, speculation has its place. Those who want to be spared the trouble of thinking, he observes, are inclined to invoke what Thomas Aquinas is supposed to have said shortly before his death — compared to what had just been spiritually revealed to him, all his writings were as old rope. Still, the order those writings brought to theological thought and not the vision is Aquinas's contribution to Christianity.[40]

So while Farrer has little use for theistic philosophy divorced from faith, the converse is also true. He was disturbed by the radical theologians' attempt to cut God down to size. The result, in his estimation, is neither more nor less than "tender-minded atheism," and his prediction is that such an anti-transcendentalism will eventually quit the game and stop talking religion.[41] Reason and religion together inform the theology for which Farrer strives, a theology in which "an entire faith is balanced by a luminous philosophical wisdom." Behind their reasonableness and candor, Farrer's books have another source of strength. Theology is talk about God, and Farrer knew what — or *whom* — he was talking about. The words he writes about God and the words he addresses to God complement each other; often they are the same. The reverence with which he is remembered at the university that was his home for nearly forty years, and the unconscious holiness that still shines in his sermons, testify to the depth of his own spirituality. "There was," Mitchell says, "a kind of transparency about him."[42] It is a perfect metaphor. It can only be added that in the best of his published work, too, Farrer achieves a transparency. Theology is for him a way of sharpening what we see darkly through the scriptural glass and the mirror of creation. It is God who counts, not God-talk.

For himself Farrer finds it best to climb the ladder from the bottom, proceeding through natural knowledge to supernatural knowledge of God, and that is the order these lectures have followed. To give revelation its preamble in rational theology is a traditional order, but Farrer thinks it a realistic order as well. "Are those Christian minds really so rare," he asks, "whose nearest gate to the invisible world is a simple awe at natural fact?"[43] The starting-point, however, is secondary. No amount of rational argument or scriptural explication can tip the scales in favor of belief unless there is an interior compulsion as well. The external factors, the creation or the story of Jesus or both interact with an internal voice. In *Saving Belief* Farrer compares conversion to the capture of a town accomplished by the combined effort of an assault from out-side and a fifth column within the walls. Success depends upon both — upon the persuasiveness of what we read and experience and upon the immediate support of the Spirit.

Where this metaphor misleads is in the fact that the town must be continually captured, because conversion never ends. Those who have found God still have God to find. Raising questions is not for Farrer an impiety, and he takes to task those preachers who avoid difficult issues, supposing that belief means a rigid dogmatism. On the contrary, our "acceptance of scripture as the word of God is not independent of an examination of the sort of thing scripture contains," and, likewise, if the God "whose name comes into our simple questions is meant as a creative om-nipotence, it has to be shown that the universe of finites allows of being interpreted as his creation."[44] So even for believers theology, rational and revealed, is part of the "external" persuasion in the never-finished business of believing.

Each of these lectures has tried to show how for Farrer theological thinking resonates with the interior dynamics of spirituality. The first considered creation as a *metaphysical* teaching. Creation is not, in other words, an occurrence to which one can point: what rational theology affirms is that absolutely everything we *can* point to points elsewhere. The natural order can only be understood as finite, unable to carry on the job of causing, and by that fact it indicates infinite causality. Yet creation is at the same time a present spiritual reality in the paradoxical awareness that "what is most freely our own is most truly God's, what is most fully our achievement is most entirely God's creation. We make ourselves what we are; but God makes us make ourselves what we are."[45]

The inspiration of scripture, taken up in the second lecture, is a more specifically Christian belief and the basis of its revealed theology. It too has a metaphysical side. To the belief that the Creator everywhere underlies the creature, the doctrine of inspiration adds that at certain points God acts in, as, and through a creature's mind — in Christian belief, through the minds of the New Testament authors. But inspiration, like creation, is also a present spiritual reality, the poetic gift of discernment by which the images of scripture fall into place. They form a pattern that seizes the mind and through that pattern the saving mystery is grasped.

Finally, the present lecture has outlined how for Farrer God's self-transcendence is both the content of the most unimaginable of Christian doctrines and also the content of Christian existence — *the* Christian experience. Creation, inspiration, and sonship are acts of God that are spiritual, immediate, and interior, as well as mediated through theological reflection on the works of God and the word of God.

Not that God has separate ways of acting. "The habit of dividing the divine government into departments is at best a convenience, and at worst a nuisance, of human speech." Farrer cannot suppose that "heaven runs a Ministry of Providence with a separate staff of angelic executives, quite distinct from the Creation Office or the Preservation Office or even (if it is decent so to speak) from the Court of Atonement."[46] These name patterns of divine activity, as do the terms justification, sanctification, and salvation. We speak of God in these ways because we must, but all of them condense or converge and aim at a unity we cannot express. God creates, provides, preserves, inspires, atones, justifies, sanctifies, saves, but God's act — which for Farrer is God himself — is eternal. The emphasis must be on the subject rather than the verbs. *God* acts. What is this act, at once creative, providential, atoning? Once more we fall into paradox; it is the act in which God goes "outside" himself and thereby draws all things to himself. And what does such a paradox mean? What content fills the formal patterns?

We can know only by experimentation, by seeking the rhythm of the Will behind all things, by prolonging it and cooperating with it, and failing and repenting and beginning again. We must, to use Farrer's word, *adhere*. In this we are not alone, for the pattern of divine Act is become a human life. This, Farrer preaches, is the offer of God: "You will create in my creation? Good: then see, I send you the Creator, through whom I made the worlds, and without whom nothing was made that has been made. I send him you in human guise, in your own form, that you may become incorporate with him, and learn, in the Creator, to create."[47] *Now therefore to the threefold fountain both of being and of grace, Father, Son and Holy Spirit, be ascribed as is most justly due all might, majesty, dominion and power, henceforth and forever.*

NOTES

ANNOTATED BIBLIOGRAPHY

List of Abbreviations

BM	The Brink of Mystery
CF	A Celebration of Faith
EM	The End of Man
FI	Finite and Infinite
FOO	A Faith of Our Own
FS	Faith and Speculation
FW	The Freedom of the Will
GND	God Is Not Dead
GV	The Glass of Vision
IB	Interpretation and Belief
LAIU	Love Almighty and Ills Unlimited
LIB	Lord, I Believe
RF	Reflective Faith
RI	A Rebirth of Images
RSJ	The Revelation of St John the Divine
SB	Saving Belief
SMSM	St Matthew and St Mark
Study	A Study in St Mark
TV	The Triple Victory

Introduction

1. J.L. Houlden, *Patterns of Faith: A Study in the Relationship between the New Testament and Christian Doctrine* (Philadelphia: Fortress Press, 1977), p. vii.
2. Ibid., p. 82.
3. *FS*, p. 14.
4. Basil Mitchell, "Austin Marsden Farrer, " *CF*, p. 16.
5. John Austin Baker, "Introduction," *EM*, p. x.
6. "A Father's Begetting," *EM*, p. 69.
7. "Human and Divine Habitations," *EM*, p. 163.
8. "Spirit and Form," *BM*, pp. 70ff.
9. "A Christian's Dilemmas (2) Piety or Happiness," *CF*, p. 129; "Remembrance Day: on Hugh Lister," *BM*, p. 117.
10. *SB*, p. 68. Reprinted by the permission of Morehouse-Barlow Co.
11. Mitchell, "Farrer," *CF*, p. 13.
12. *GV*, p. 53.
13. *SB*, p. 6.
14. Mitchell, "Farrer," *CF*, p. 14.
15. "Responsibility for Our Friends," *BM*, p. 60.
16. "Prologue: Theology and Philosophy," *RF*, pp. 2-3.

Chapter I

1. *GV*, p. 147.
2. *GV*, p. 3.
3. *FI*, 2d ed., p. ix.

4. "The Rational Grounds for Belief in God," *RF*, pp. 10-11.
5. *FI*, p. 6.
6. "A Moral Argument for the Existence of God," *RF*, p. 127.
7. *FS*, p. 10.
8. *FS*, p. 15.
9. "God and Verification I: The Nature of God as Personal Act," *RF*, p. 139.
10. Bonaventure, *The Soul's Journey into God*, trans. Ewert Cousins, The Classics of Western Spirituality (New York: Paulist Press, 1978), pp. 56, 60-65, 79, 87.
11. *GV*, p. 66.
12. *GV*, p. 8.
13. *GND*, p. 34.
14. Evelyn Waugh, *Decline and Fall* (Little, Brown & Co., 1977), pp. 38-39.
15. *FS*, p. 114.
16. *GND*, p. 93.
17. "Transcendence and 'Radical Theology,'" *RF*, pp. 173-174.
18. "Does God Exist?", *RF*, p. 43.
19. *GV*, p. 94.
20. *FS*, p. 116.
21. *FW*, p. 315.
22. *FW*, p. 300; see also "Freedom and Theology," *RF*, p. 170.
23. "Moral Argument," *RF*, p. 118.
24. "Moral Argument," *RF*, p. 120.
25. *BM*, pp. 122-123.
26. *FW*, p. 309.
27. *GND*, p. 100.
28. *SB*, p. 124.
29. *SB*, p. 30.

30. *EM*, p. 143.
31. *SB*, p. 121.
32. *BM*, p. 126.
33. "Grace and the Human Will," *RF*, p. 198; see also *GND*, p. 101.
34. *FS*, p. 122; see also "Moral Argument," *RF*, p. 130.
35. *FI*, p. 60.
36. *GND*, p. 70; emphasis added.
37. *BM*, p. 3; cf. *FS*, pp. 130, 143.
38. *FOO*, p. 216.
39. *GV*, p. 130.
40. G.K. Chesterton, *A Second Childhood*, quoted by Eric Mascall in *Existence and Analogy* (London: Longmans, Green and Co., 1949), p. 85.
41. *LAIU*, p. 12.
42. *LAIU*, p. 15.

Chapter II

1. *CF*, p. 58.
2. *FOO*, p. 89.
3. *EM*, p. 75.
4. *GV*, p. 39.
5. *FOO*, p. 180.
6. *GV*, p. ix.
7. *GV*, p. 35.
8. "Poetic Truth," *RF*, p. 24.
9. *FS*, p. 99.
10. "Inspiration: Poetical and Divine," *IB*, p. 41.
11. *GV*, p. 99.
12. *GV*, p. 44.
13. *GV*, p. 105.
14. *RI*, p. 13.

15. *RI*, p. 13.
16. *EM*, p. 109.
17. "Poetic Truth," *RF*, p. 29.
18. Dorothy L. Sayers, "Towards a Christian Aesthetic," in *Christian Letters to a Post-Christian World*, ed. Roderick Jellema (Grand Rapids, Mich.: William B. Eerdmans Publishing Co., 1969), p. 80.
19. *GV*, p. 115.
20. "Poetic Truth," *RF*, p. 34.
21. "Theology and Analogy 2: Knowledge by Analogy,"*RF*, p. 70.
22. "Poetic Truth," *RF*, p. 35.
23. "On Looking Below the Surface," *IB*, p. 55.
24. *Study*, p. 9.
25. "The Mind of St Mark," *IB*, p. 21.
26. *CF*, p. 41.
27. *Study*, p. 25; cf. pp. 8–9.
28. *GV*, p. 36.
29. *Study*, p. 30.
30. *RI*, p. 16.
31. *GV*, p. 140.
32. *SMSM*, p. 114.
33. *Study*, p. 245.
34. *SMSM*, p. 10.
35. "Inspiration: Poetical and Divine," *IB*, p. 43.
36. *SMSM*, p. 12; see also *Study*, p. 88.
37. *GV*, p. 109.
38. *GV*, p. 44.
39. *GV*, p. 41.
40. *FOO*, p. 111.
41. *Study*, p. 226.
42. Based upon *GV*, pp. 139–145.
43. *GV*, p. 139.
44. *GV*, p. 137.

45. *EM*, p. 11; see also *Study*, p. 208.
46. Quoted in John D. Crossan, *The Dark Interval: Towards a Theology of Story* (Niles, Ill.: Argus Communications, 1975), p. 23.
47. *GV*, p. 145.
48. "On Looking Below the Surface," *IB*, p. 64; see also *Study*, p. 53.
49. *SMSM*, p. 202; see also *Study*, pp. 67–68.
50. *SMSM*, p. 19.
51. *SMSM*, p. 35.
52. *SMSM*, p. 106.
53. *Study*, p. 52.
54. *EM*, pp. 11–12.
55. "Can Myth be Fact?", *IB*, p. 167.
56. *FOO*, p. 114.
57. "Inspiration: Poetical and Divine," *IB*, p. 53.
58. "Revelation," in *Faith and Logic*, ed. Basil Mitchell (London: George Allen & Unwin, 1957), p. 103.
59. *GV*, p. 36.
60. "The Inspiration of the Bible," *IB*, p. 12.
61. *RI*, p. 22.
62. *TV*, p. 11; cf. *GV*, p. 61.
63. "The Inspiration of the Bible," *IB*, p. 11.
64. *CF*, p. 66; cf. *EM*, p. 75.
65. *GV*, p. 41.

Chapter III

1. *GV*, p. 78.
2. "Can Myth be Fact?", *IB*, pp. 170ff.
3. *Study*, p. 251.
4. *Study*, p. 264.
5. *CF*, p. 66.

6. "Myth," *IB*, p. 173.
7. "Myth," *IB*, p. 173.
8. *CF*, p. 94.
9. *FOO*, p. 39.
10. *CF*, p. 148.
11. *Study*, p. 287; *CF*, p. 94.
12. *Study*, p. 288.
13. *Study*, p. 289.
14. *FOO*, p. 102.
15. "Very God and Very Man," *IB*, p. 128.
16. *SMSM*, p. 11; cf. *GV*, pp. 110–111.
17. *TV*, pp. 24–25.
18. *CF*, p. 23.
19. *TV*, p. 9.
20. *GV*, p. 48.
21. *GV*, pp. 41, 109.
22. *CF*, p. 74.
23. *LIB*, pp. 9–10.
24. *LIB*, p. 23; see also "The Prior Actuality of God," *RF*, p. 180.
25. "Messianic Prophecy and the Preparation for Christ," in *The Communication of the Gospel in New Testament Times*, Theological Collections, no. 2 (London: SPCK, 1961), p. 6.
26. *SB*, p. 100.
27. *CF*, p. 103.
28. *LIB*, p. 38.
29. *LAIU*, p. 125.
30. *FOO*, p. 112.
31. *FOO*, p. 16.
32. Daisetz Teitaro Suzuki, "Crucifixion and Enlightenment," in *Mysticism: Christian and Buddhist* (New York: Harper & Brothers Publishers, 1957), pp. 129, 133.
33. *CF*, p. 169; Augustine *De civitate Dei* 8. 17.

34. *FOO*, p. 23.
35. *EM*, p. 60.
36. *SB*, p. 105.
37. "An English Appreciation," in *Kerygma and Myth*, ed. H.W. Bartsch (London: SPCK, 1953), pp. 222–223.
38. *FOO*, p. 187.
39. Basil Mitchell, "Austin Marsden Farrer," *CF*, pp. 14–15.
40. *FI*, p. 4; "The Christian Apologist," in *Light on C.S. Lewis*, ed. Jocelyn Gibb (London: Geoffrey Bles, 1965), p. 32.
41. "Transcendence and 'Radical Theology,' " *RF*, p. 177.
42. Mitchell, "Farrer," *CF*, p.13.
43. *GV*, p. 96.
44. "Introduction," Michael C. Perry, *The Easter Enigma* (London: Faber and Faber, 1959), p. 12; *FS*, p. 13.
45. *CF*, p. 147.
46. *SB*, p. 53.
47. *BM*, p. 94.

AN ANNOTATED SELECTION OF THE WORKS OF AUSTIN FARRER

An asterisk (*) indicates books that are in print

A. PHILOSOPHICAL THEOLOGY

Finite and Infinite: A Philosophical Essay. 1st ed. London: Dacre Press, 1943; 2d ed., 1958. Reprint. New York: Seabury Press, 1979.

The second edition of this, Farrer's first full-length study, differs from the first only by the inclusion of a new preface in which attention is drawn to certain difficulties Farrer had come to see in his original argument. It remains, however, a classic in metaphysical theology, three hundred pages of unrelentingly difficult — and equally brilliant — philosophical theism.

The Freedom of the Will. 2d ed. London: Adam & Charles Black, 1963; 2d ed. New York: Charles Scribner's Sons, 1960.

This book, which contains the Gifford Lectures for 1957, has a wider scope than its title suggests. "All the most vital topics of philosophical concern," Farrer writes, "come into the argument," of which the second edition provides a useful summary. Only the last of the fifteen chapters is explicitly theological. It concentrates on the importance of free voluntary activity — the reality of which is argued in earlier chapters — as a clue to knowledge of God's activity.

God Is Not Dead. New York: Morehouse-Barlow Co., 1966.

This book is the same as the one published in England under the title *A Science of God?* It is an excellent introduction to Farrer's arguments for theism. Intended for general readership, it sacrifices nothing of the main lines of his mature thought.

Love Almighty and Ills Unlimited. New York: Doubleday & Co., 1961.

A book which contains the Nathaniel Taylor lectures for 1961, this is Farrer's most extended work on theodicy — the justification of belief in an omnipotent creative providence against arguments that such belief is incompatible with the presence of physical and moral evil in the world. Farrer's approach here is thoroughly philosophical and thoroughly Christian.

B. SCRIPTURAL DIVINITY

A Study in St Mark. London: Dacre Press, 1951.

St Matthew and St Mark. 2d ed. London: Dacre Press, 1966.

The first of these two studies presents Farrer's initial attempt to lay out the imaginative patternings by which the earliest evangelist gave symbolic expression to what Jesus Christ did and meant and was. The second study combines revision, expansion, and recantation. Farrer writes that its properly descriptive title would be "the pattern of St Mark's Gospel, and of St Matthew's in so far as it throws light on St Mark's, with a few hints from St Luke's."

*A Rebirth of Images: The Making of St John's Apocalypse. London: Dacre Press, 1949; Boston: Beacon Press, 1963; Gloucester, Mass.: Peter Smith, 1970.

The Revelation of St John the Divine: Commentary on the English Text. Oxford: Oxford University Press, 1964.

The case with this pair of books is similar. The first, which is the only one of Farrer's biblical studies still in print, presents arguments about the complex and imaginative imagery of the last book of the New Testament. The second makes some substantial revisions and simplifications without, however, altering the main points of interest. Farrer was somewhat constrained by the commentary form, and A Rebirth of Images remains in many ways the better of the two.

C. COLLECTIONS AND GENERAL STUDIES

*Faith and Speculation. New York: New York University Press, 1967; London: Adam & Charles Black, 1967.

This "continuous reflection on theistic belief" is Farrer's last book. Although it is partly a reworking of his arguments in the much earlier Finite and Infinite, there is also a consideration, from a philosophical standpoint, of "revelation and history." Faith and Speculation is a significant statement of Farrer's mature thinking on the empirical approach to theology; because it began as a series of lectures, it is in some ways more readable than others of his scholarly works.

The Glass of Vision. London: Dacre Press, 1948.

This book, which contains the Bampton Lectures for 1948, is undoubtedly the most important source for understanding the breadth of Farrer's genius. It considers the function of images in poetry, metaphysics, theology and scripture — all in order to illuminate "the form of divine truth in the human mind." Both St Mark and St John, the New Testament writers Farrer studied most extensively, are discussed, as are the themes of voluntary action, analogy, and aspiration.

*Interpretation and Belief. Edited by Charles C. Conti. London: SPCK, 1976.

Those who seek a brief introduction to Farrer's thought have cause to be grateful to C.C. Conti, who collected and published the essays in this volume and the one listed next, as well as many of Farrer's sermons. This collection contains a number of studies in specifically Christian theology: essays on biblical themes, the Virgin Mary, the doctrine of justification, and others.

*Reflective Faith: Essays in Philosophical Theology. Edited by Charles C. Conti. London: SPCK, 1972; Grand Rapids, Mich.: William B. Eerdmans Publishing Co., 1974.

These essays treat in narrower scope themes developed in *Finite and Infinite, The Freedom of the Will,* and *Faith and Speculation;* there is also an essay on "Poetic Truth" closely related the *The Glass of Vision.* The editor has assembled at the end an exhaustive bibliography of Farrer's published work.

Saving Belief. New York: Morehouse-Barlow Co., 1965; London: Hodder & Stoughton, 1964.

Written for undergraduates, this "discussion of essentials" excellently fulfills its purpose and brings together rational and revealed theology in a readily understandable, but never simplistic, manner.

D. SERMONS AND DEVOTIONAL WORKS

A Faith of Our Own. New York: The World Publishing Co., 1960.

The sermons here, collected by Farrer himself, are slightly Americanized but otherwise identical to those in *Said or Sung* (London: Faith Press, 1960). The British version does not have C.S. Lewis's introduction, and the pagination is different; it does include several of Farrer's poems, omitted from *A Faith of Our Own.*

Lord, I Believe: Suggestions for turning the Creed into Prayer. 2d ed. London: The Faith Press, 1958.

Here Farrer develops his conviction that "prayer and dogma are inseparable." The book incorporates an earlier broadcast talk suggestively entitled "The Trinity in Whom We Live."

The Triple Victory: Christ's Temptations according to Saint Matthew. London: The Faith Press, 1965; New York: Morehouse-Barlow Co., 1965.

Written as the archbishop of Canterbury's Lent Book, this is one of Farrer's most successful interweavings of biblical scholarship and deep devotion. The first chapter especially shows clearly how his scriptural divinity has its roots in meditative reading.

A Celebration of Faith. Edited by Leslie Houlden. London: Hodder & Stoughton. 1970.

The first posthumous collection of Farrer's sermons presents, in some ways, the cream of the crop, including his learned Hulsean Sermons. Also to be found here are Farrer's translation of the *Veni, Creator Spiritus* and the memorial address given by his friend and colleague Basil Mitchell shortly after Farrer's death.

*The End of Man. Edited by Charles C. Conti. London: SPCK, 1973; Grand Rapids, Mich.: William B. Eerdmans Publishing Co., 1973.

*The Brink of Mystery. Edited by Charles C. Conti. London: SPCK, 1976.

These two collections comprise sermons unexpectedly found by their editor while "rooting around under the rafters" of Katherine Farrer's attic-loft. Though somewhat uneven, each collection contains gems.

The Crown of the Year: Weekly Paragraphs for the Holy Sacrament. New York: Morehouse-Barlow Co., 1953.

$3.95

AUSTIN FARRER's criterion for theology is "an entire faith . . . balanced by a luminous philosophical wisdom." His work includes provocative biblical studies and carefully reasoned arguments for belief in God. At the same time, he was one of the outstanding preachers of his generation. To all of the many facets of his writing, Farrer brings a deep Christian spirituality. "It isn't a choice," he insists, "between following the reason and trusting the heart. It is a matter of putting heart into a rational conviction, and bringing mind into the heart's devotion."

JACOB'S LADDER introduces Farrer's philosophical theology, his sermons, and his scriptural divinity, stressing the unity among these seemingly isolated pursuits as well as their common ground in practical religion. In an age of scholarly specialization and theological fads, Farrer's vision of what reflective Christian faith is deserves to be more widely known.

Cowley Publications, Cambridge, Massachusetts 02138